Faithfully Yours

The Letters of Byron Herbert Reece

Edited by
Raymond A. Cook and Alan Jackson

Cherokee Publishing Company
Atlanta, Georgia

Books by and about Byron Herbert Reece

by Byron Herbert Reece

Ballad of the Bones and Other Poems
Hardcover ....978-0-87797-100-9 .... $17.95

Better a Dinner of Herbs (Novel)
Hardcover ....978-0-87797-101-6...........$25.00

Bow Down in Jericho (Poetry)
Hardcover ....978-0-87797-102-3...........$25.00
Paperback ....978-0-87797-310-2...........$16.00

The Hawk and the Sun (Novel)
Hardcover ....978-0-87797-103-0 ....$25.00

The Season of Flesh (Poetry)
Hardcover ....978-0-87797-104-7........... $17.95

A Song of Joy and Other Poems
Hardcover ....978-0-87797-105-4 .... $24.00
Paperback ....978-0-87797-309-6 ....$15.00

by Raymond Cook

Mountain Singer: The Life and the Legacy of Byron Herbert Reece
Poetry and Biography of a Hill Country Genius
Paperback ....978-0-87797-246-4 ....$14.95

Available from your favorite bookseller or

Faithfully Yours

The Letters of Byron Herbert Reece

Byron Herbert Reece

Edited by

Raymond A. Cook and Alan Jackson

Cherokee Publishing Company

Atlanta, Georgia

Library of Congress Cataloging-in-Publication Data

This book is printed on acid-free paper which conforms to the American National Standard Z39.48-1984 *Permanence of Paper for Printed Library Materials.* Paper that conforms to this standard's requirements for pH, alkaline reserve and freedom from groundwood is anticipated to last several hundred years without significant deterioration under normal library use and storage conditions.

Manufactured in the United States of America

ISBN: 978-0-87797-374-4

Design by
Kenneth W. Boyd and Pamela Haury Kohn

Cover Photo Courtesy of
Hargrett Rare Book and Manuscript Library
University of Georgia

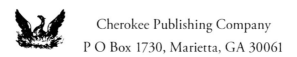

Cherokee Publishing Company
P O Box 1730, Marietta, GA 30061

Acknowledgements

We want to express our appreciation to all of those persons who generously gave or made available the letters or portions thereof which follow.

Preface

At this writing, it has been forty-nine years since Byron Herbert Reece's tragic death at forty years of age. Yet before his death, critics had nationally and variously acclaimed him as follows:

> I know of no living poet writing in the English language who has written lyrics equal to the best poems in *The Season of Flesh*. It seems to me that with the exception of Robert Frost, Reece is our greatest poet, and even Frost is not so pure a lyricist, nor as strong and lonely a voice.[1]
>
> He was a genius among us ... who contributed something of value, something that will live when the highly acclaimed here today and gone tomorrow trash of our phony geniuses is gone.[2]
>
> The ghost of Sidney Lanier may haunt me ..., but for me the greatest poet who ever lived in Georgia was a mountain farmer named Byron Herbert Reece.[3]
>
> On the same day that Byron Herbert Reece's book [*The Season of Flesh*] was published, there was also published a new volume of verse by W. G. Auden. I chose to tell you about *The Season of Flesh*. Auden is of course a great "influence" on poetry, but Reece is a Poet born.[4]
>
> [Reece is] ... one of the really great poets of our time, and one who stands with those of any other time.[5]

---

[1] Edward M. Case, quoted in Ralph McGill, *The Atlanta Journal-Constitution*, February 20, 1955.

[2] Jesse Stuart, "Byron Herbert Reece: In Memoriam I." *The Georgia Review*, XII (Winter 1958), 361.

[3] Bernice McCullar, "Lonely Farmer in the Hills was an Outstanding Poet," *The Atlanta Journal*, May 28, 1966.

[4] Edward M. Case, "'Season of Flesh' Proves Reece As Towering Poet," Syracuse, New York, *Post-Standard*, February 13, 1955.

[5] Ralph McGill, *The Atlanta Journal-Constitution*, July 13, 1951.

Similar appraisals could be cited at great length. If these appraisals of Reece are accurate, the question naturally arises: Why is Byron Herbert Reece not better known? The answer seems to lie within these considerations – the current popular critical taste, the personality of Reece, and the sad circumstances of his life, and the fact that his works had been out of print for a number of years until 1985. Neither by action nor appearance did Reece strike his acquaintances as being different, or pretending to be different, from what he was – a mountaineer farmer who seemed to hold that silence is better than speech, that character is better than appearance. His face was pinched and craggy and reminded some of his friends of portraits of the young Abraham Lincoln. Most of the time his hair hung unregarded over his forehead, and his face had that impassivity one associates with rural mountain folk. On occasion a remark by someone in his hearing would provoke a startled, frightened look which vanished almost as soon as it appeared. He was a man notable for his long silences, but these silences were all the more appreciated by his friends, because when he broke those silences everything he said sounded important in a quiet, subdued way and should be carefully attended. He baffled many people of casual acquaintance because, as he said privately, he had "no horse to ride." When he was poet-in-residence at U.C.L.A. and at Emory University, or when he made public appearances, he sensed that people were trying to see what made him tick, or to determine what he was "after." It was incomprehensible to many people, that he could be just exactly what he appeared to be – a mountain farmer, a man who moved about among his mountain neighbors as one of them.

When Reece could be enticed out of his valley to read his poetry, he did not try to be clever or witty in the after-dinner-speech tradition and usually would plunge immediately into the quiet, deep waters of his poetry. When he finished he would sit down in a shy, abrupt way that strangely moved his listeners. By the established canons of public speaking, Reece was not a particularly good reader of his own poetry, but to those who knew him, his natural shyness and hesitant modesty in reading aloud the expressions of his deepest feelings were memorable and moving. As one listener put it, "It raised one's hackles to come smoothly and dreadfully to the climaxes of his ballads. It chilled the blood to listen to the clean, cool line of sentience and sadness in his lyrics." [6] Though in his maturity he maintained a correspondence with a few persons truly dedicated to creative writing like himself, he had no affinity for the commercial world of letters or the mutual-admiration circles of literary society. So naturally did Reece blend into the hills from which he derived his inspiration that it is now difficult to visualize him anywhere else, for, as he once said, his closest kinship was with "laurel and

---

[6] Elizabeth Stevenson, "Byron Herbert Reece: In Memoriam II," *The Georgia Review.* XII (Winter 1958), 363-364.

rhododendron and granite." The fundamental integrity and authenticity of the man and poet are bases upon which his unique contribution will ultimately rest.

Growing up in an isolated mountain region, Reece had little external stimulus which other people interested in literature could have provided. He had therefore to struggle alone through his early years, pursuing his goals in loneliness. But his passion for words was with him from his earliest years. He had read *Pilgrim's Progress* and much of the Bible before he even started to the little Wild Boar School to and from which he walked seven miles each day. He tells later that the Baby Ray Reading Books at the school seemed somewhat less satisfying so he spent much of his time listening to the recitations of the higher grades in the one-room school. His stimulation in the early years came almost altogether from the Bible and the works of the great English and American poets who had preceded him. In a letter dated December 1, 1940 he wrote to his friend Philip Greear: "I'll wager I have read the work of more poets than any other person in the South." To those who knew Reece in his maturity, his statement carried no hint of egotism, it was simply the truth. He must have read millions of words by lamplight, by fireside light, and finally by the electric light which came to his home on Wolf Creek. During his teens in the long winter nights, he would carry a kerosene lantern to bed and read as many as four books at a time. A number of critics have remarked that Reece was the best-read person they knew.

Though Reece attended Young Harris College, a Methodist institution in the North Georgia Mountains, he left without being graduated because he refused to take the French courses, which he considered an affectation. Nearly twenty years later he remarked that it still irritated him to come across a French phrase in a perfectly good English sentence. Reece later took a rather sardonic satisfaction in the fact he was invited to be poet-in-residence at Young Harris, Emory, and U.C.L.A. even though he was not "qualified" to teach in the lowest grades of public schools.

Reece's novels exhibit the same care and workmanship of his verse, but it is likely that Reece thought of himself as a poet, first and always. Indeed, his novels are carefully wrought poems, for in the phrasing, tone, and direction of his sentences there is the delicate and muted irony, the jolting effect upon the heart at truth suddenly laid bare, and the brooding, ineluctable sadness which characterizes his lyrics. His four major volumes of poetry are *Ballad of the Bones* (1945), *Bow Down in Jericho* (1950), *A Song of Joy* (1950), *and The Season of Flesh* (1954). The novels are *Better a Dinner of Herbs* (1950) and *The Hawk and the Sun* (1955). All of these were published by Dutton, whose editors said they would take anything he wrote, though they lost money on every one of his books.[7]

---

[7] All of these titles were reprinted by Cherokee Publishing Company in 1985.

In the years following his brief student days, Reece continued to publish widely in periodicals, ranging from the *Prairie Schooner* to the *Sewanee Review;* he taught briefly in the little mountain school; lectured as poet-in-residence at three institutions of higher learning; published four major volumes of verse and two novels; received the Georgia Writers Achievement award several times for the most distinguished writing in the state; received several votes for the Pulitzer Prize for both *A Song of Joy* and *Bow Down in Jericho*; and won several other awards, most notably two Guggenheims. Such achievements by many another writer would have been more than sufficient to establish for him a firm reputation, but the retiring personality of Reece was so marked that he never bothered to capitalize on his gains. He characteristically remarked in a letter to a friend that he seemed to have missed the publication of *Bow Down in Jericho*, for it came at a time when he was too pressed to pay any attention to it.

In 1950, when Reece was invited by U.C.L.A. to conduct courses as poet-in-residence, he faced the prospect with mixed feelings. Coupled with his extreme disinclination to "exhibit" himself as a poet was a desperate need for money. He had the care of his elderly and tubercular parents, and the small farm had produced poorly the season before. His misgivings about the trip to California were expressed in a letter to E. V. Griffith, dated April 28, 1950: "I may not get on well with the highbrows at U.C.L.A. If not, I'll be living by myself at the extreme end of the campus, and should be able to avoid them much of the time." After his arrival, he wrote Griffith on June 20: "I feel as if the Summer Session may take all of the sap out of me if I have to cope with Ph.D.'s the whole term."

Reece returned home tired and nervous. His notebooks reveal the meticulous care he gave to preparing his lectures, most of them written out in full. The long, hard hours on the farm, plus the late hours he kept for correspondence with a few friends and for working on his writing until 3 A.M. dragged him down further, and he began to have that vision of what lay ahead for him. In a letter to Philip Greear in November 1951, Reece wrote: "My father will probably go to a sanitorium [sic] soon, my mother won't agree to go. I'll probably end up in one myself ... " Reece's need for living expenses was helped to some extent when he was invited to be poet-in-residence at Young Harris College, but this experience only tired him more because he gave more time to the students than his health could bear. By February, Reece was in Battey Hospital, the state tuberculosis sanitarium at Rome. The months he spent there were nightmarish for him, and he later said that if he ever wrote about his experience he would call it "A Chronicle in Hell." He could not bear to see those around him suffering, and one morning in April, still far from recovery, he simply put his clothes on over his wasted frame, walked quietly out of the hospital, and headed for home.

While he was trying to recover at home, his mother died of tuberculosis August 1954. Her death, whose coming he had silently and solemnly watched for months, plus the realization of his own possible future, lent a growing somberness to his work and letters, and he became even more withdrawn. During this period it seems that certain psychic foundations had shifted, and he began that long poetic soliloquy of disturbed thought which was not to cease till death. He, like the youth in a poem of Housman's, saw his path and where it led. But in spite of his illness, he exerted himself to keep a lengthy correspondence with a few cherished friends, especially younger writers who wrote to him for guidance.

By 1956 he had sufficiently recovered to teach at Emory University as poet-in-residence. But the specter was always before him as he intimated to Edward Pratt Dickson in a letter dated April 4:

> I'm in fair shape as regards that [his illness], only always have to be careful, always have to be careful and worry about whether I'm being careful enough until I reach the point of to hell with it. I sometimes wonder if I'll ever have guts to write anything else of any consequence. Maybe, maybe not, I can't feel that it matters.

Reece concludes the letter in this manner:

> It is spring here now with the service trees and the red buds in bloom. A little earlier the wild plums, with their bitter-sweet odor. At this time of the year I always get nostalgic for eternity. Did I ever define nostalgia for you? It is the instantaneous recognition of our mortality.

The following summer Reece was again teaching at Young Harris College, but in a letter of June 17 to Elliott Graham at Dutton's he writes with an edge of desperation in his words:

> Well, I've just reached my wall. I've reached the absolute limit of my energy. I couldn't do more than I'm doing if my life depended on it. That's all there is to it. I think perhaps you might be right in thinking things would work out in time. But waiting it out is a luxury that I cannot afford anymore. Well, to hell with it. I've got to eat. I don't like to be hungry. So I'll meet my English classes as long as I can.

In the spring of 1957, Reece received a second Guggenheim award which would enable him to devote full time to writing a new novel that he planned to call *The Ax and the Sword* and would concern itself with the settlement of his mountain region. With misgivings, Reece decided to work on the novel at the Huntington Hartford Foundation (a subsidized colony for artists, musicians and writers) near Pacific Palisades, California, because the foundation had offered to pay Reece's living expenses. This reluctance to go out into the world again was expressed in a letter of May 5 to Pratt Dickson:

> I have lost contact with most of the people who meant anything to me in earlier years. I have now stopped getting involved with people. In the words of the prologue of the *Hawk* [*The Hawk and the Sun*] etc., I am committed to the knowledge of the insuperable separateness of the individual. It was better, though, when an illusion spanned the distance between me and the individual.

He planned originally to be at the Foundation through the following winter, but in a letter to Pratt Dickson on July 14, less than a month after arrival, he wrote: "This is not my climate really. I think I'll have to get back on the ground, North Georgia and vicinity, before I can do much with the novel … " At the end of the letter Reece concluded: "I miss the open countryside of Georgia."

There must have been some fateful urgency to return to his beloved mountains, for when the fall term opened Reece was back at Young Harris College. The academic year 1957-58 must have been a tortured one for him. His closest friends had the impression that he saw himself becoming a burden upon others, and though he might with proper care live a year or so longer, he would not be able to produce the work to which he had dedicated himself. We shall probably never know fully the answers, for there was a sense of heroic pride in Reece, sometimes exasperating to his friends, that made him fight his battles in silence. A few close friends thought that perhaps Reece's loneliness was made piercing by the knowledge that he would never be able to marry and have a family. We only know that he seemed to be more withdrawn and nervous, he had developed a tremor, and his personality had deteriorated to such an extent that he intimated a sense of panic at the thought of meeting other persons, and seemed to be at relative ease only when he was in the safety of his room.

There were times when he came to the dining hall at the college under the influence of alcohol. Late one night in May, he went impulsively to Dr. W. F. Tanner at the college clinic where he was given a sedative and put to bed, but before dawn the next morning, for reasons known only to himself, while the mists still hung over Brasstown Valley, he slipped out quietly alone, never to return. Byron Herbert Reece had made his last appeal to medicines that cure the flesh.

On June 3, 1958, on the eve of graduation exercises, Reece seemed to be greatly agitated. He had earlier in the day said he had attended about all of the graduating exercises he could stand. That evening he appeared at the dining hall with the appearance of having been drinking. After a caustic remark concerning the food, he left almost immediately without eating anything. At 10:30 that evening two students, Ken Kirkpatrick and Bob Carpenter, came running to the apartment of Mr. Fred Edmiston, director of the dormitory Hamby Hall, considerably agitated, saying that they had just left Mr. Reece in his apartment in Peel Hall where he had seemed strangely detached. Mr. Edmiston immediately ran to the apartment of Dr. Howard Hanson, a good friend of Reece's, to see what might be done. Dr. Hanson impulsively thrust a carton of ice cream into Edmiston's hand and asked him to take it immediately to Reece in the hope that Edmiston might have an excuse to go to Reece's apartment and possibly avert what the students had feared might happen. Edmiston ran as rapidly as he could to Peel Hall, but his mission was too late, for when he arrived at the apartment and opened the door, he found Reece lying full length on the floor with a bullet symbolically through his left lung. In the drawer of his desk were his final examination papers, graded and neatly stacked. His phonograph was just completing a Wanda Landowska rendition of the Mozart *Piano Sonata in D.* Professor W. L Dance, who had been a major influence in directing Reece as a student toward the highest ideals of literature, had killed himself in that same room several years before. Maybe it was only coincidence, or perhaps Byron Herbert Reece in his action saw fit to make on that spot his last obeisance and acknowledgement to his beloved teacher.

Once when Reece was urged by E. P. Dutton to leave his farm and move near the center of literary activity in New York so that his name and work could be better publicized, he replied that he could wrestle with his angel at one Penuel about as well at another, and if he should persist without ceasing, he might even prevail. On the night of June 3, 1958, Reece wrestled one last time, and the angel won.

Nowhere does Reece reveal his intense personality more compellingly than in his letters. It is significant that he would often unburden himself to a correspondent three thousand miles away more readily than he would one three feet away. Although Reece on occasion confessed to being bitten by "the spider of immortality," it is not clear that he ever expected his letters to be published. In correspondence with the newspaper columnist Celestine Sibley, he remarked concerning the published correspondence of Edna St Vincent Millay:

> I find the letters revealing and interesting for the light they throw on the writer's life, but very few of them are outstanding as letters. I suspect Millay would claw at her coffin boards if she knew the letters had been published.

He further adds:

> I rest in confidence that nobody shows such lack of judgment as to preserve my letters for posterity.

Apparently nearly all of Reece's correspondents would not agree, for many of them expressed satisfaction and pride in having kept Reece's letters with the conviction that they were preserving the account of a unique personality who deserved to be better known and appreciated. Such was apparently the case with Ms. Sibley, who concluded:

> The personal correspondence and the diaries of Thomas Jefferson, Benjamin Franklin, and yes, Miss Millay herself, are far more fascinating than any biography could be. The same is true of the gifted and tragic Byron Herbert Reece. [8]

Though this collection of letters is not comprehensive, it will contribute to a greater understanding of such a complex and intriguing writer. And, we hope that this collection – along with the newly founded Byron Herbert Reece Society, an oral history of Reece sponsored by the Reece Society, and an ever-growing body of scholarship – will add to a renewed interest in the man and his literature, and will provide a wider appreciation of his legacy to his state and nation.

---

[8] This quotation and the two preceeding by Reece are included in Celestine Sibley, "Hardness of Life Shows in the Letters of Byron Reece," *The Atlanta Constitution-Journal,* July 13, 1965.

YOUNG HARRIS COLLEGE
YOUNG HARRIS, GEORGIA

January 14, 1940

Dear Leon [Radway]:

To amuse myself I have fallen so low as to copy light verse on toilet paper and disfigure my walls with it. Some of it is fairly good, for instance this limerick I got from Prof Dance.

There was a young lady of Siam

Who had a handsome young lover named Priam.

When he asked for a kiss

She said, "I'll resist

But god knows you are stronger than I am."

I take turns liking and hating my classes. I enjoy the poetry course, for one reason I never have to read the lesson, and for another reason I enjoy Bob. Half the time I wouldn't give him a free ride to hell, and at other times I could almost love him like a piece of statuary or a fine painting or something of that order. I know nothing whatever about him and I don't expect to learn anything about. I don't want to any more, I enjoy him more as it is.

And as far as I am concerned the whole shooting works can miss fire. I hate the whole conglomeration. They head me off in every direction; they force me to be the biggest hypocrite under the sun; vanity, vanity, all is vanity saith the preacher.

I feel slightly defeated and unclean, as if I hadn't had a bath in a long while. I read three books last Thursday for the express purpose of forgetting things around me for awhile. Naturally the books were short. Wilder's *Our Town*, Millay's *Fatal Interview*, which I had read before, and a *Book of Hours* by Culrose Peattie. But they didn't help me very much, I need you to stabilize me again, you unconsciously, or was it unconsciously? … did that about once a week.

Here is the *Echoes*. I must have been out of my head to let them use such a moronic looking photograph at the head of the column. That and the title which is not mine, by the way, is enough to scare off all readers, even if it were not something on the order of literature, and nobody reads literature if they know it. You were my public and I don't enjoy the column anymore.

If I have anything published that I think you'd like I'll send you a copy.

So long

Feb. 1, 1940

Dear Leon:

I have had a slight case of flu and used it as an excuse to go home for a while. I hate this place anyhow. So I didn't get your letter until today. I couldn't send your trunks COD by the bus so I went to Mr. Moore's office and he said I could send them by the Axley Truck lines. That is what I did. Mr. Moore said if the truck did not deliver them to your house they would notify you when they arrived at Axley's depot, wherever it is, I didn't bother to find out since if they don't deliver them to you, they'll let you know where they are in Atlanta. Mr. Moore said the truck would pick them up tomorrow at his office. I hope they get there all right. I addressed them thoroughly, and fastened them as well as I could. I put your overcoat, bathrobe, tennis racket, and a few other articles in the trunks. If there is anything left out let me know and I'll see if I can find them. So much for that.

I had a fire in my room a few days ago, or last week sometime, I don't remember when it was, anyhow all the damage that was done was done by the firefighters and not by the fire. They completely tore away one wall and so I have been homeless ever since. They practically demolished my books, I wouldn't have minded mine so much but I had Bob's *Christ in Concrete* and it was damaged too. My typewriter was open on my table with part of an article in it, plaster and water gummed the damned thing up until I had to take a day off and take the thing piece from piece and clean it up. It still doesn't work so very well. The H sticks and some of the other letters have a tendency to jump. Somebody stepped on the case and bashed in one side, I straightened it out however. I have been forced to sleep wherever I could find somebody who would sleep with me, or rather, let me sleep with them. I hate to sleep with most folks with a purple passion (I mean I hate to sleep with anybody with a purple passion. Damn it to hell, I mean for "purple passion" to modify the verb hate.) It's hard sometimes to make words say what you want them to, but it's good exercise at least.

There is a ball game in session just outside the window from the room I'm in. If the nincompoops wouldn't yell their silly selves hoarse I wouldn't mind them so much. Do you remember the only ball game I attended last Quarter? I did it on your account, though God knows it was not your fault that I went. I guess I merely went because you did. There was nothing wrong with going of course, I just didn't enjoy it.

I have six poems in the latest *Poetry World* but I'm so damned poverty stricken right now I couldn't buy enough air to live at a penny a cubic mile. You have seen most of them anyway, they are: "Precaution," "Nursery Rhyme," "In

Orchards Hung With Fruit," "If Evil Were A Little Road," "Futile Errand" and "Couplet." I have fifteen pages of book reviews in the same issue, but they couldn't possibly interest anybody as creative work; they only serve the purpose the buyer needs, tell (sometimes the reviewer is right, but mostly wrong) whether the book is worth buying or not. I don't buy books anymore, so I don't take the trouble to read the reviews, not even my own.

I hope Bob and I get down to Atlanta sometime during Feb. Bob said he might go down to Agnes Scott when Robert Frost comes to lecture, and that if he did I could go with him. If we do it will be at night. If I don't get to come, I wish you would hear Frost's lecture and tell me what you think of him. He is one of my favorite Am. poets. I wonder though, can the son of so and so speak.

The paper should have been out last Monday, but it isn't out yet, I expect it out tomorrow. I'll send you a copy when it comes out. I feel like the top of my head were going to float off, I actually was not very sick when I went home. I guess it will be poetic justice if I do get sick now.

Always,

____

YOUNG HARRIS COLLEGE
YOUNG HARRIS, GEORGIA

Dear Leon:

Anything written from here must be repetition since nothing ever happens, but by rehashing the normal little episodes of living from one miserable day to another you might make it readable, in case you had the genius of Thomas Wolfe to whom nothing was important, and nothing was unimportant. I have been reading *Of Time and the River* and it makes me furious. He takes up about thirty pages to describe the actions of three people waiting for a train, normally the action would take just about as much time to happen as he takes to tell it. I grant him that he is damn good, or rather he was, for now, as somebody has it, "he takes his wages in the dust," but why in the name of God take so much space to show it.

For no good reason I'm tired, but it's not unpleasant, I could lie still for hours and not be bothered by a thing in the world. I don't think when I'm tired, and so I suppose the moral is stay tired, or drunk. I went to Jacksonville the other night and drank almost a quart of wine and grape brandy, I felt fairly well the rest of the night. However, such procedures do not help my self respect any. The natural estate of man is one of at least a healthy capacity for enjoyment, and if he bitches up the arrangement let him take the consequences. Actually I am not as ill natured as I appear on paper. But why bother to tell you since you know it any way.

Here is a poem by Millay I found the other day in some book.

Butterflies are white and blue
In this field we wander through.
Suffer me to take your hand.
Death comes in a day or two.

All the things we ever knew
Will be ashes in that hour.
Mark the transient butterfly,
How he hangs upon the flower.

Suffer me to take your hand.
Suffer me to cherish you
Till the dawn is in the sky.

Whether I be false or true

Death comes in a day or two.

I think maybe we are having a renaissance in the Quill Club. Maybe the anthology will be out by the last of March. If it's not good I will be thoroughly disappointed. I have existed these last few months for you and a chance to work on that damned anthology. I am just selfish enough to get all my own work in it I can, as Lieberman says, "it's dog eat dog and let the weak beware." By the way the last column in the *Echoes* was a disgrace, it stinks to high heaven, and to make it worse the type setter misspelled both the title and incandescent in my poem. I advise you to destroy it. I could have you put on the mailing list but having had some experience with that honorable branch of the publication, I know that the chance of receiving the paper is practically nil, so I'll continue sending it myself. I though of dedicating a poem to you in the column, , but for it to mean anything to you I would have to expose myself to these morons whose chief delight is prying into other people's affairs, and I don't intend to give them an opening.

I have attempted to write some poems, but they ended in the wastebasket, leaving me furious and hating myself and everything within reach. I recognize the symptoms from previous experience and I am not too concerned about the whole affair. I will finally arrive at the point where creation will follow its own will, and I'll bring order out of chaos. This is merely the price I have to pay for the enjoyment the finished product gives me. I promise you, if I live long enough, a book neither to your discredit nor mine, I may suffer from it but I don't mind that, after a period of hatred of myself and my work, and I usually do my best work under such conditions, I feel washed out inside. If there is anything I worship it is cleanliness of body and soul, though I am sadly lacking in both.

Actually though I think you should be worried about me. I walked to Bald last Saturday with the temperature ranging but a few degrees above zero. Sarah went with me, which proves she hasn't very much sense either. But I got a lot of animal satisfaction out of it, so why not?

Life for me begins about two o'clock, it's very close to that time now but I slept through breakfast, as usual, attended two classes, and then slept through hash and well into the fifth period. I have poetry that period and usually get there barely in time for Bob to make a fool of me. That's not a difficult job, especially when I'm sluggish with sleep. I have more fun in that class than in anything else. We are undoubtedly the dumbest crowd under God's heaven. The class is a travesty and Bob will flunk the whole shooting works, and what is more do it with a clear conscience, and I won't blame him. I don't expect to flunk the course since most of the test questions are about the technical aspects of verse and I have not studied that for seven years for nothing.

Bob said he spent most of last Friday afternoon with you. He feels about as lost without you as I do I think. Since I have begun to consider him simply as a human being I am forced to revise my opinion of him. I used to hate him so thoroughly that the emotion was almost physically painful. The error was mine and is so admitted.

If you come to the banquet you will be here before you answer this, more than likely. I hope you do come, you know that as well as I do.

I'm shaking so from cold that it's difficult; to keep my equilibrium, I think that is one syllable short, but what are the odds in such damnably cold weather?

I'm taking you at your word, and am much relieved for it.

So long,

____

BYRON HERBERT REECE
BLAIRSVILLE, GEORGIA

April 21, 1940

Dear Leon:

Time is such a relative matter I forget where I am within it. Whereas spring was undeclared when you were here, now the leaves are about half grown and the fields are becoming green; there is as much difference in the landscape now and a week ago as between the seasons of winter and summer. Spring is a hard season but I like it most of the four. Frankly I enjoy it, work and all, and if I am sentimental I make no apology; there should be a few things top-side of God's earth that a person is permitted to enjoy without thrusts from the worm-eaten cynics, spreading their green poison upon the bread of life. I am rural by nature and raising as you may have noted, and outside of nature I take very little enjoyment from creation. I hate very few people, and love less, but the majority of them are no more to me than so many trees, and certainly none are as beautiful-not that trees are objects to turn your heart over. (A good subject for some narrow brained scholar would be to trace down the philosophy that first seated emotion in the heart.) I have been plowing for two weeks, there is nothing romantic about that, rather few things are more monotonous than following a plow around and around like a fish in a bowl. Even the few attractions do not offset the tiresomeness of the work. Though it sounds all right to say it's fine to watch distance grow ribs, to participate in the growing is something else again. To the observant there are any number of things to watch-it takes no attention to plow-but I forgot to see what there is to see. I did, however, come unexpectedly upon four snakes all in one pile indulging in the primal fact of procreation. At my advance the slimy creatures all belly up to the mouth slid quickly into the water; but like dogs engaged in the same business they were hung; and it amused me to watch one dragging the other through the clear water. My interest was not that of a naturalist, rather it was superficial and interest at all because it was the first time I had watched such an incident. And once this afternoon about five o'clock turning at the end of a land I happened to look toward the west, and the sun at such an angle upon the water had turned it to pure silver. Each ripple flowed unbelievably upon the other as silver as anything has ever been. I take time out from my own cynicism to take note of such incidents. Added together they make a sum, of sorts, of experience free of the body's action and thus uncontaminated by the human failings … seeing you unexpectedly made clear a few things and muddled many more. It made me conscious of how much I have missed you; and considering my carelessness of dress, which though in nowise affected is abbeted(sp) by lack of funds(A kindly way of putting poverty, though I am immensely better off than a lot of people) and lack-luster habits it set me wondering what in the hell you would do with me in Washington. Though I have no doubt but that I could adapt myself to the city, I have no desire to do so, and as for formality I hate it almost as passionately as possible without going to the trouble of trying to do something about it. I think most young people at one time or other invent a desire to remake the world, but I was cursed with enough sense to know I couldn't do anything about it, cheating myself of the activity of the crusader; which is about all I'm fit for. I am firmly convinced that the world is going to the dogs, what of it that has not already arrived, and long ago I began a campaign, not to divert it from its destination, but as much dog as the rest, stay behind and snap at the heels of those who are going faster than I am. I have a book in my head I'll do sometime called *Congregation of the Lord*, and I'll do it too, if I live long enough; I finally get around to doing all that I intend, though sometimes I am years about it. You can imagine what it will be, I think, knowing me as you do. Another I am going so write will concern you and me, but it won't see print for years yet and there'll be time enough to explain it, if there'll be time enough. I am going to be absolutely truthful sometime before I die if I don't die too soon and unexpectedly, and the result will be worth looking at, though I'll make certain I'm safe and dead before it is seen ... but I'm wondering, (substitute a for o and you'll have what I mean). I thought of you on the way home until I hit a sharp rock on that damned new road and a tire blew out. I cursed the rest of the way ... I've got prices from almost every printing concern in America, and sample volumes, in most cases, and the lowest price I can find for a decently printed and bound book in an edition of two hundred copies is $130 dollars. I am going to find out what an edition of one hundred copies will cost and then proceed ... I'm going to dedicate my book to you, not because of material aid from you, but because I would have anyway. Which means something or other that you can figure out for yourself. Not that I would be casual about it. I don't feel that way at all ... My third story will soon be in print, and I find them so easy to give away, much easier than verse, that I may try to sell some soon ... I promised to send you a copy of the first and subsequent ones, and I will finally ... by the way did you get your copy of the *Citizen*? That promise was fulfilled earlier than most of mine, but be of good cheer, to quote Paul, I'll get around to the others unless the proverbial green-eyed monster slips up on me, and it that case it would make no difference one way or the other.

Faithfully,

Herb

BLAIRSVILLE, GA.

May 15, 1940

Dear Leon:

Boy, what has happened to you? I wrote you twice, rather I sent you a paper and a short note, and then I spent the better part of a night writing a three page letter, I hope all that letter has not been wasted on the Dead Letter office, or in other words did you get it? I know there must have been some postage due on it.

So for a week I expected to hear from you, and the next week I spent feeling hurt, as I had a right to do, but this is the third or fourth week and still no answer.

Seriously though, why have I heard nothing from you for so long? If you are merely unhappy, so am I, as usual, and that's not a very good excuse for not writing.

There has been little out of the ordinary at YHC. Bob has been ill, with a heart attack, I think, he is better now. The QC anthology is in the hands of the printer, it will be out about the 25th. I'll send you a copy when it's out. By the way I'm using *Mother Hubbards* in a group of three Nursery Rhymes, dedicated to you. I'm contributing a poem a week to the *Union County Citizen,* published at Blairsville. I'm submitting a book of poems in the *Kaleidograph* book publication contest. It closes at the end of the month. I feel lucky, not that I can thrust my feelings.

Two issues of the paper are enclosed; I think that brings them up to date. There'll be one more issue.

When may I expect to see you at Y.H.C., if I may expect to see you there? The champion debate is June 10th.

The tree of silence may bear the fruit of peace, but I well doubt it … and I think you have heard that before somewhere. Have you ever considered what an ass I was then? If you have not, for God's sake don't.

But for my sake write, actually I have been pretty badly worried about you, or rather, about myself should your silence indicate that your interest in my direction had ceased.

Always,

Herb

P.S. I said I was sending two copies of the paper, but I can't find a copy of the last issue. I'll send it Thursday, and no lying this time.

BLAIRSVILLE, GA.

June 30, 1940

Dear Leon:

I'm sending the manuscript in miniature since that will save postage all the way around, besides it is easier to handle in this form. After it has been read all the way around, if it is to be published I'll retype it, make whatever revisions are necessary, and look after the punctuation more strictly. Notice I said <u>if</u> it is to be published.

These poems are enough to fill a pamphlet. There are two more I will include when one of them comes out *Poetry World*, and I get another copy of the last issue of *P. W.* I don't have copies of them otherwise. They are: "All The Leaves In The Wildwood" and "As I Came Down." A pamphlet is the only sensible form of publication in this case. A book would sell a little better, but there's a great deal of difference between eighty and two hundred and fifty dollars, unless you are rich.

Whatever faults the poems have, lie not in the poems but in me. I may want to change a word or so but otherwise they are as good as I can make them. To change any of them would be to write a new poem. They are numbered as I want them arranged. They seem to form something of a sequence in this order. I'm sending a page of a pamphlet that has the terms of publication.

And as for us, I'm impossible I am beginning to realize, but you are pretty difficult yourself. But I can change my mind as easily as I can my pants, more so in fact, since, as E. A. Robinson once said, my pants hang over my damned heels. (This typewriter makes me furious; it doesn't operate worth a tinker's damn.) I suppose you had better not come after me for a while. Beside just naturally hating to inconvinence, that's the third time I've misspelled the miserable word, and I do know how to spell it, (inconvenience) anybody, in case I like them, otherwise I don't mind at all; I'll be pretty busy farming until my school starts. I'll pay my own way to see you with my first check. The sentence is a little involved, and damn this paper.

You might try writing me, even if I do lose my temper and what small sense I may have. I'm afraid you are a little too important in my scheme of things.

BHR

P.S. I'll title the pamphlet later.

8/27/40

Dear Leon:

I suppose by now you have inferred that I am the biggest liar under the sun, and I freely admit it. This letter is some five weeks late and for the best reason that I have ever had: teaching school. Do I like it? O yes, very much, is my usual answer, but you would know better, so speaking truthfully, I hate it down to the last detail. Christ said of children; of such is the kingdom. Then, Good God deliver me from heaven, which he probably will.

I board with fine people as far as that goes, but invaders from space would have to come round the back way to get here, I keep expecting to fall off the edge of the world here, and if some monster from ages long dead should come upon me suddenly I wouldn't be surprised. So much for that.

For the last week or so I have been listening to some good music. I have access to a radio, for a wonder, and I've put in good time using it. I heard the "Finale" from the *New World Symphony,* "On the Trail," from the *Grand Canyon Suite,* and best of all, the "Gypsy Dance" from *La Boheme,* or however in hell you spell the damn French title. I guess I should ask forgiveness for mentioning such pieces to you, but you know me well enough to know that I really like them: I wouldn't take the trouble to assume a pose for the kings of all the countries of the world. Damn their lousy hides.

Some day I am going to have to ask you to destroy all my letters. You could ruin my reputation, what little I have, very easily. And under one condition I wouldn't care: that yours went along with it so that you would have to share my exile or disgrace, or what have you. And why I got to mumbling on this subject I can't imagine, unless it is that I have to watch my language and all the other little things that I am lax in, around my pupils. Actually, could you imagine me teaching school? One day I told the students they could go. Where to, one boy wanted to know; and before I could think I told him he could go to the devil as far as I was concerned. That could have cost me my position, but I had no complaints. And I was fiddling with an acorn and a bright little nut told me that only hogs ate acorns, I threw him the acorn and told him to finish it. His mother was furious. They try to trap me into answering foolish questions. One boy asked which was right: I am a fool, or I is a fool. Either in your case, I told him. It's hard to keep from hating them, and yet I know that I once had their attitude toward teachers. I can manage them on a human basis, and make them like me, when I can get one to himself; then I cease to care whether or not they like me and all's to do again, as the very great, and very much dead, Mr. Housman would say.

And whipping: Good God, I hate to beat on their flesh, but if I didn't whip some of them, I couldn't get in a mile of the schoolhouse. I refuse to whip girls. I make fun of them, which makes them cry and serves the purpose of a whipping. One of the fifth graders is eternally betting I can't pick him up and so forth, and I have to take him up on it; and then He (damn the capital) gets into something and I have to beat on a warm a sensitive back that I can almost span with my hand. To hell with the whole business.

I will be in Atlanta on October 6, for the day only, or for part of the day only. I'll come down on the bus and Marel Brown and her husband will meet me at the station and take me to the Meltons where I will have to read some poems and speak for about twenty-five minutes, so she says. I'm damned if I do. At least she says I am to be the honor guest of the Poetry Forum of the Atlanta Writer's club. Why Mrs. Brown added honor, is quite beyond me. By the way, she is paying my transportation. Do you see any way for me to see you during that time? I had rather have an hour or so with you than with the Poetry Society of America, but didn't you once say something to me about making contacts? Damn them anyway. O yes, I had a very nice and lying letter from Daniel Whitehead Hickey. Could you imagine that?

I think I would like Naugle. I've not had a chance to hear him read poetry yet. But I'll have to stop. It's dark. I intend to send you some poems, but don't look for them until they arrive. I'm tired of breaking promises.

As ever,

Herb

10/22/40

Dear Leon:

Well, I could hardly expect you to be in a good humor concerning me after so long a desertion. But I had reasons, too many and too unpleasant to recall. My father almost died from a hemorrhage along about the time I should have written you, and then I was so busy doing hard labor, too hard, to do anything but eat and breathe what it took to keep me alive. Then I renigged on the Poetry Forum for the simple reason that I was too tired and sick and discouraged to go to Atlanta, no offense meant to your damned unholy city. You should have received an invitation to the affair, I asked Mrs. Brown to send you one. Did you go?

The invitation is still open and I may take the dear lady up on it some time. I won't say when, I guess you are becoming tired of my unintended lies.

I am now teaching again. It makes no difference to me whether the people like me or not — except for one reason, I may want to teach again next year, the political boss of my school has asked me if I would teach here again. I don't know whether I will or not. It is not important but for the simple fact that I can use the money, God, can I! I have exactly nineteen cents from my first check of sixty dollars. But I don't know what has become of it.

You said you had a beautiful copy of *Leaves of Grass*, well, there's plenty to think about within the covers, even if the author did mumble a great deal about the "love of comrades." The poor fool had neither the taste for normal love nor the nerve to indulge in homosexual love. But that is beside the point. I wish you would pick me up a copy of it. I'll pay you for it. By the way, get me a copy of Daniel Whitehead Hickey's *Wild Heron*, which will come to the Atlanta markets about the 25th, or a little later. Mr. Hickey has been kind enough to brag to me at some length of his contract with Harpers to bring out his next three books. But he is really good, so more power to the egotistical runt.

I have a brand new copy of the *Oxford Book of English Verse*. Harold Mikell, the white headed guy that T. Jack kicked out after the strike gave it to me last Sunday. What have I done for him to deserve it? Listened to him blow off his mouth without blowing mine off in return.

I have eleven poems in the last issue of *Poetry World.* I wish I could afford to send you a copy. They are the best I have had published to date. You might find a copy for sale at Millers bookstore. My first story will come out in the winter number of the *Aerend*, published by the Kansas State College. I'll see that you get a copy of it, just for the hell of it, because it will be my first prose published with the exception of about twenty thousand words of book reviews.

You understand, or should, that I do not force my literary activities upon you for the sake of my ego, but in exchange for something that I value a hell of a lot, your friendship, and my meager success in the literary world is about all by which I can justify myself.

By the way, quit burning your candles at both ends, you won't last long enough, and I want you to last a great deal longer yet, I've scarcely seen you, you know, in the last several months.

Faithfully,

Herb

11/6/40

Dear Leon:

Now that the die is cast for the next four years, I suppose our ears can rest from all the political bull. I had no preference, being of so little consequence that I would not be affected. You berate me in good round fashion in your last letter. I deserved it of course, and plan no retaliation. If you understood how I hate to copy that I have already labored over you could see now I have not already sent you copies of my junk. Don't offer to let me back down, I won't do it. By the way, if this seems ill natured, don't take as such, it isn't at all. And I say this for the last time, so if you ever want affirmation of it reread this: You have become a part of my way of living, not to be easily rooted out, whatever [?]ertion you my suffer on my part will not be more than a seeming one. I suffer from a failure of the spirit every now and then, and while it lasts I respond to nothing. In such a state I might desert you for a while <u>but I always return what I have assumed as mine</u>.

I wish you wouldn't take the world so hard, it's wormy I grant you, but for God's sake don't have your body fighting that from which there is no escape, <u>except by spending the body</u>. I have forgotten my text.

I will copy the poems and send them to you about ten at a time. I may write some comments on some of them in order to make them more intelligible. By the way, if you happen to run on a copy of *Poetry World* for the months of March, April, May, June, and God knows how many more month: they are all combined in one issue, please pick it up for me. I have eleven poems in it and don't have a copy. There are no more copies with the publisher, and I have no copies of the poems in it. So you see how it is.

So Long,

BHR

By the way, do you know what has become of the ms. of The [?] if you will get it from [?] you may have it. I guess I have forgotten [?] of what should have mentioned.

BHR

BYRON HERBERT REECE
BLAIRSVILLE, GEORGIA

2/26/41

Dear Leon:

I'm sorry I've been subjecting you to my horrible script, but I got tired of typing. If the last letter was not clear here are the main points: I want to have a sixty64four page book printed in an edition of a hundred or so copies. That will cost somewhere around fifty dollars, if an additional hundred copies are printed the second hundred will cost about seven or eight dollars. Thus if the book should sell at all the second hundred would be somewhat more profitable than the first. The point at all is somewhat obscure. I think that by sending review copies to only the best poetry magazines and a few critics that are not just space writers we could get some honest criticism and publicity. The limited edition would place it in an apocryphal position, that is, it would make each copy of more value than it would be otherwise. Just the old law that makes gold and diamonds of more value than sand. Most reputations are matters of showmanship. I'm not a good showman, but I think it would be no trouble selling enough copies to make the investment back. As far as the contents of the book is concerned I'm not much worried. I have enough poems of a quality as good as I can make them to fill one volume. It would contain all that I wouldn't care to let the moths have, should I kick the old proverbial bucket, or take a bayonet in my guts, as I probably will if the two-faced so and so who signs himself president continues to kick freedom in the pants and assumes Hitler's britches.

So that is that, if it's anything. I don't see why you bother with me. I'm merely thankful that you do, not thankful to the Lord, since He doesn't seem to have much to do with it, but grateful to you. I won the *Charlotte Observer's* poetry prize last week. I don't know which of three poems won it, but they were all new.

I feel like a full sized battle were raging in my chest. If I don't have pneumonia I'll be surprised. I've escaped the flu so far, but now I'd as soon lose a tooth as take a step. However I've felt this way before and nothing came of it, if I can outface those damned brats for a few more days I'll be all right. Meanwhile-

Faithfully,

Byron Herbert Reece

1 Dec, 41

At Leaf Fall

Dear P. G. [Philip Greear],

Elucidation be damned. Don't change your sonnets. Let brother Hewitt acquire a little imagination. I can't say as I know exactly what you are talking about, but the drift is satisfying enough. I had meant to write you a long time ago and tell you to add a little hard work to your genius, and be patient, and you would come out on top. I mean that; don't let anything but lack of time stop you from producing, and that only as long as absolutely necessary. And don't be lucid. For God's sake, there is much too much lucid tripe cluttering up the universe now. You are out of danger on that score, I think. I am not. I <u>can</u> write lucid, goody verse, God forbid; and though I never want to, my ability to do so betrays me at times, I am not as good as I used to be. I can't write lyrics anymore except for rare slip-ups. I have been writing ballads for almost a year now. Four of them have found publication in *Prairie Schooner*. Another will be out in Dec. in the same mag. Jesse Stuart wrote me about one of them. He said "Fox Hunters of Hell" was the best ballad by an American he had read. I know better, of course, and you would too, but such stuff helps to bolster my ego. I'll send you a copy of the next *Schooner*. I have had other verses in different publications. How come I don't know, but I can send second class stuff to the publications that have been publishing me for years, *Kaleidograph*, etc., and they will keep on publishing me. By the way, a poem of mine from *Poetry World* has been used in a college textbook called *English Patterns*, published by Ginn. I was invited to submit stuff to *New Republic's* supplement "Writers Under Thirty" but I have not heard from them yet and don't know how I came out. But that's too much about me. You are neglecting the best field for your type of work. The quarterlies published by the colleges are better suited to your brain children. I don't advise you to send stuff out to the lesser known verse magazines, since their standards are rotten, but why not try *Prairie Schooner*, 12th & R Streets, Lincoln Neb. *New Mexico Quarterly Review*, The University of N. M., Albuquerque; *Modern Verse*, Box 4002, Albuquerque, is also an excellent publication. *Wings*, Box 332, Mill Valley, Calif., is also a good magazine, and receptive to thought. But I'd try *Schooner* with the sonnets. And I think you might make some of the quality Mags. Especially if you would study them and submit work not too out of line with their usual run. I don't mean you should slant for anybodys damned standard, but there are reasons and reasons why etc., you must have access to several good magazines in so large a camp. If you sign your offerings to the pay mags. with your rank etc, it will help, for as the old song goes, "there's something about a soldier."

I am still unhappy at school teaching as I would be at anything more than likely. I hate to stay in a school room all day, hate it to such an extent that I get nervous and snappy like a big dog confined to a narrow cage. But I don't know as I'll be teaching much longer. The TVA damn, I spelled it that way on purpose, has about moved all my students away. I had an average of about six last week and that ain't enough, not by a long crack. But at least I don't have to contemplate three years as yet, and that's something as even I realize without having to experience it. Winter is almost upon N. Georgia. The leaf that hangs from the lone bough of autumn is brown now, no longer red or yellow. And I don't go to YHC anymore, except once I went to meet Broadrick. Broad works in Southern and Citizen's in Atlanta. That is as close as I have even a friend that don't speak my language. You are scarcely more isolated in that respect than am I. Of course I can sit here at home and listen to WQXR to my heart's content. That is the NY station that has good music from daylight till twelve. And since they broadcast at ten thousand watts now I can get them perfectly at night. I have seen Dance twice since he left. I miss him more than I would have the remainder of YHC. The Quill Club is still going under the direction of Dunaway and Bob Lance; but you would not recognize the idea you dreamed up in its new garb. Rather than tarnish a beautiful memory I avoid the QC. I'm going to quote you two recent poems. One which says nothing but lacks nothing, and one that lacks something, though God knows what. The first is called "Rural Air." (And is based on an old weather prophecy)

When the wind goeth round
The rain will fall,
And a dripping sound
Be heard by the wall.
Love, is that all
When the wind goeth round?

Happen a kitten
Will sleep in the hay,
Ant the mule be bitten
By flies and bray.
What else, Love?
Who can say

When the wind goeth round?
Chance our love
Will sicken and die
Like some sick dove,
Not knowing why?
Neither you can say, nor I;
For love will alter
And life blow by
As the wind goeth round.

And the second produced by an absolute stillness of landscape and weather on a frosty morning that you would appreciate. I have yet to find a title.

Thin vapor in this listless air
Lifts like a misty ghost of thought
Into the concave morning where
The dull coin of the sun is caught.

A breath of air drifts out from whence
The wind has not the strength to rise,
And frost upon the elements
Lies like a sleep on buried eyes.

As if to presage what is found
When sleep arrests us foot and head
The day lies still beneath spent sound
Hung perilous and dead.

Now you tell me what.

As ever,

BHR

BYRON HERBERT REECE
BLAIRSVILLE, GEORGIA

April 1943

Dear Philip:

Do you remember Millay's "Earth does not understand her child"? You see I have a text for every occasion, however imperfectly recalled. The point is right now that I do not understand my friend. I have always been under the impression that I am a very ordinary human being, granting me a few exceptional traits like my exceptional frankness, up to a certain point. I am an extremely democratic person; too, you know in what sense I mean. And otherwise I am very dull to myself. All this you must understand is brought about by your sentence: disturbing I say for there is ... etc. I have had the same complaint from one other person who used to be a close friend in my high school days, I never see him now. How disturbing? In what way, that is, not to what degree.

But to get down to matters of importance to you, "Paebar" is all right, very good in fact. And *Poetry Digest Annual* is standard in its field. When you get the book let me know what is your critical opinion of it. I was once represented in it but have never seen a copy. Where did the sonnet appear in the first place, and will you make me a copy? I have not seen it and want to. And now I shall lecture you a little: your poetry is of a quality not as once obvious to the reader which is unfortunate only inasmuch as most individuals are mentally lazy and put a premium on obviousness. But don't worry, you will arrive; but the road is hard. Now let me say that you should in no way try to make your work of a character other than it is to <u>you</u> for that is as it should be. I'll wager I have read the work of more poets than any other person in the south; this is not egotism, it is true, and I have watched poets emerge from obscurity to somewhat of a place in the sun, and who, do you think, came out on top? The difficult poets, for on the whole they have more to say; that is a very good one reason why they are difficult. My own work, as Swallow tells me, depends for its success on an extremely fine phrasing, which I occasionally pull off. It lacks a natural complexity. One reason is that to me poetry is chiefly lyrical in nature. I can think complexly sometimes but I do so in prose; and when I do in poetry it is always through analogy. Well.

The night after your visit I was in a mood, and I always write when I am in a mood. I wrote a twenty-six stanza ballad, "The Ballad of the Rider," which has been gone to *Atlantic Monthly* ever since. It shall be returned no doubt but I will send it elsewhere for it is as good a ballad as I can write. A second ballad of mine of the same length will be in the fall *Prairie Schooner*. And Sunday following I invented, I hope, a new form. It is an abbreviated form of the sonnet. A not too good example:

After a season when all love was lost
To earth turned carrion and to sea turned blood
A poet wandered where the iron*shod host
Had wheeled in battle in an ancient wood
The boles were blasted but the stumps remained,
An eloquent symbol to the thinking mind
Of conquest thwarted, and of victory gained.
He hurried on with dreadful need to find
The changed earth changeless as it used to be,
And found it where, full to its ultimate shore,
The appointed tides raised up the heavy sea,
And the little brooks ran quietly, as before.

You can see that it is nothing but three quatrains, akin to the sonnet only in the thought division. I have written several in the form and contemplate a sequence to see if it really is worth anything.

Now, will you tell me what you think of "Of Men and Roses"? I am considering whether to include it in a manuscript I may submit to *Kaleidograph's* book contest. It seems to be the favorite of the former members of the QC, Gaskin, etc, but I am afraid, to paraphrase, they are in Rome and thinking with the Romans, it was Dance's favorite of all my junk. And will you send me the address of *Voices;* I happen to remember that the address as given in the list you have is different from the old address, which I have. Don't return the list, just give me the address.

Too long a separation? I am as I was, and when the trump sounds the little worm that spews me from its belly will know it is.

Act accordingly.

Byron Herbert Reece

BYRON HERBERT REECE
BLAIRSVILLE, GEORGIA

Oct. 4, 1943

Dear Philip:

I'm glad to hear from you. I'm glad too that you have had acceptances from *American Poet.* I'm so damned poor that even $0.10 per line seems a heaven-send but encouragement is worth more at times. I hope you follow those poems, whatever they were and I'll be getting copies of them, with Athens. The *Am. Poet* is, and rightly so, partial to service men. So you have an outlet for your poetry if you will develop it. Get me say this, you have the makings of a really fine poet, don't for God's sake be led away from poetry. I am not a flatterer, I mean what I say.

A bookstore would be fine for you and Mildred, I am sure. I would like the atmosphere of a bookstore myself, but I doubt if I have the patience to deal with customers.

Dutton's have asked to see a complete manuscript of mine, and I am working tooth and toe nail to get one together. They were very encouraging in their letter, but I am still hoping with my fingers crossed.

I don't know how long I shall remain a civilian, but I hope you come to Helen before I am [?], of and when.

I hope you'll forgive [?] a letter, I am usually very prolix as Cellini would say. But I must get back to typing my ms.

Faithfully,

———

P.S. Can you conceive of anybody writing a letter while listening to Schubert's "unfinished"? This is Sunday; I merely dated the letter for tomorrow since that is when it will be mailed

BHR

RFD # 1
BLAIRSVILLE, GA.

November 29, 1943

Mr. Fred T. Marsh

E. P. Dutton & Co.

New York, N.Y.

Dear Mr. Marsh:

I am happy to comply with your request to send you additional poems, and to tell you something about myself. I shall mail the poems within a day or two, meanwhile, since there is little to tell about myself and the telling won't require much time, here are some facts about my life. I feel that it is only fair to warn you that I am new at this, and I hope you do not expect too much of me.

I was born in 1917, on a farm in North Georgia. The district in which I was born is called Choestoe, which is derived from the Cherokee Indian language and means "the dance of the rabbits." I still live on a farm, and only a mile from the one on which I was born. I live between Blood Mountain and Enotah Bald, the two highest peaks in Georgia. There is a nice Indian legend about blood, and De Soto is supposed to have named Enotah when he passed through this country. A state highway now runs through our farm, through Neel's Gap to Gainesville and Atlanta. By the way, I have always been a little angry about the name of Neel's Gap. Before the highway came the gap bore the name of Frogtown, or more properly Walasiyi, which is Cherokee for "the place of the frogs." Neel was merely the engineer who selected the route for the highway. I have never been able to see why we should have sacrificed a perfectly good place name for that of a mere man. It was years after I was born, though, before the highway was built. We were quite isolated then. The old country road came to our place, butted up against the base of Blood and stopped. We went to church, about three miles distant, to mill and to the store in a wagon. When I started to school I walked seven miles, there and back, each day. I can remember very well when my father used to haul pork to Gainesville, fifty miles away, in a covered wagon. He required four days to make the trip. I once went with him to Cleveland, the nearest railroad station, after a load of fertilizer. We were two days on the road, we slept in the wagon at night; and it was on this trip that I saw my first train.

I attended the local school, off and on, until I finished the seventh grade. My mother taught me to read before I entered school. I had read *Pilgrim's Progress* before I ever set foot in a schoolhouse. I thought it was a fine fairy tale, and I've thought of Bunyan's Masterpiece as a fairy tale ever since. I graduated from the local high school, with second honor in a class of nineteen, in 1935. I couldn't manage to raise enough money to go to college, so I stayed on the farm until 1938. I had a poem in the July 1938, issue of the *American Mercury;* and the president of Young Harris College, a junior college, gave me a three-month scholarship. Later I worked on the college working gang, and proved to my own satisfaction that working your way through college isn't as noble as it is generally cracked up to be. I finished two years at Young Harris but I didn't take a diploma because I avoided math and flunked a course in French. I didn't see the use of so many verb forms. It makes me pretty angry to run across a French quotation in an author's work.

I taught in a rural school for two years. I hated it thoroughly. Since the Spring of 1942 I have been farming. I had a llc deferment this year but it has run out and the draft board probably has plans for me in the fairly near future.

I am getting a little vague about it now, but I think my first poem to be published appeared in the August 1937 issue of *Kaleidograph.* Henry Harrison published a large number of my poems in *Poetry World.* I have since had poems in most of the "little" magazines. I sold a poem to the *American Mercury* in 1938, but soon after Palmer sold the magazine to Spivak, and I have not been able to sell Eugene Lyons anything. I have never submitted to any of the other quality magazines with the exception of *Va. Quarterly Review* and once to *Atlantic Monthly.* Lately I have been selling poems to the *American Poet,* published in Brooklyn and to *The Poetry Chap-Book,* published at 227 East 45th Street, in New York City. I have sold one poem to the *Washington Post,* and have submitted nothing else to them. The Ballads in my collection *Ballad of the Bones and Other Poems* have all been published in magazines, with the exception of the title ballad. It is to be published by *American Poet,* and I hope to win a prize with it in their current contest. "Monochord" is the only poem is my collection in your hands that has not been published or accepted for publication. You may use it as you see fit.

As I have stated, I shall send a number of additional poems within one of two days. And may I say that the acceptance of my collection by E. P. Dutton & Co. is the most important thing that has happened to me since September 14th, 1917, when I first beheld the light of day!

Sincerely Yours,

Byron Herbert Reece

January 7, 1944

Dear Pratt Dickson:

I hope you are good at reading script. You'll need to be to make head or tails of this. I usually use a typewriter-but at the moment I am down with a severe cold and my sinus is giving me trouble to boot. I merely note this to explain why I am submitting you to this cryptogram. I don't feel up to sitting at the typewriter.

I am happy that you like "If God Should Need Me." I rather liked it myself, though as a usual thing I have no feeling for my own stuff after the fever of creating it passes. It says something of what I wanted it to say. That is a rare thing with me—a poem is never realized completely. If I could make a poem convey what produces it in the first place, I would be a success—true poet indeed.

I am going to comply with some of your requests—I don't exactly know why. I always acknowledge every letter I receive, since that is common courtesy, but I never write out poems in longhand; and I've received hundred of poems to criticize since the first publicity about my book came out. These I've returned with only a very general criticism. But I'll be glad to look over anything you care to send me—only not too many at once, please. I warn you that I don't pose as a critic at all. I think I know good work when I see it, but that's merely my personal opinion. To get back to the reason for my departure from my rules—it may be because you are 21—I'm 28 and this appears to myself ancient compared with you. It may be because you are obviously a very sincere lover of the land, and I have run across so few of them, and I suppose it's partly because I admire you for sticking to your guns and going to school on your own efforts. I worked on a college farm myself a few years ago.

I'm enclosing a copy of "If God Should Need Me"—It will be the only one in existence since I don't have the original handwritten copy—I usually destroy them after they are copied on the typewriter. I'm also sending you a copy of a pamphlet I had published in 1944. There is a copy of "Music I Heard" enclosed—so it saves me the trouble of making you a copy. I'll send you a copy of *Ballad of the Bones* when one is available again—the 1st edition is exhausted and it has gone into a 2nd printing. This too is a departure, for I'm too poor to give away many copies.

Faithfully,

Byron

BLAIRSVILLE, GA.

January 9, 1946

Dear G. B.

In the words of one of Tennyson's poems "I am a-weary, a weary." I have a terrible cold, and a sinus affliction-in short I am in no mood to write a decent letter but I have for the time being to ration my time and work whether I feel like it or not.

I am going back to Atlanta to be honor guest at "a Baptist Beanfeast," in the words of Frank Daniel- or in other words, to a luncheon of the Atlanta poets at the Druid Hill Baptist Church. Unfortunately I'll have to read some of my own junk to the public in the church auditorium. While I am there I'll look up the big fellow Eugene Jones. I don't know whether he was really large or whether the whiskey and soda I didn't drink had gone to my head.

How do you like Miss.? I've been re-reading some stuff by Faulkner, and native of that state who writes pure horror at times-and if his portrayal is anything like a true one I am happy that I'm a native of the much maligned state of GA.

My friend Rapnay is back from the wars; I've also had a letter from our friend Gaskin. He is an Ensign, and is at the Phila. Navy Yard. Crawford is at Yale; T. P. Watson has a church at Savannah Beach. G. [Gordon] Thompson was "confirmed" by the recent N. Georgia Conference. The various and sundry people who touched our lives at YHC keep writing to me about *Bones*. I'm glad to hear from them, of course.

"Or ever the Golden Bowl be Broken" must have been very personal; and for you alone. I have no copy of it. I do remember it, however.

If you get back to GA, soon I wish you would let me know. I'd like very much to see you.

By the way, the "Curtiss House" burned last week. I shudder to think of the effect on poor old Mrs. Curtiss.

Faithfully,

Reece

BYRON HERBERT REECE
BLAIRSVILLE, GEORGIA

Toward the last of March [1946]

Dear G. B. [George Broadrick]:

Let us hope this turns out better than the last letter I wrote in your direction. The odds in favor of it are considerable, because I feel at the moment like one made over. It is a funny thing, but when I have been writing too hard, and have accomplished something maybe, I feel weighed down by a sense of futility. But I have been working like the proverbial nigger on the farm today and there is certainly nothing futile about that. I plant, and what I plant grows. God and I do pretty well with growing things. (God to me is a companionable sort of person, sometimes, though at others he eludes me completely ... and I'm not going off my nut either; I've always felt this way about things but the publication, or I should say the reception of *Bones* has stripped some of my false facades from me.) (In other words, since some people seem to find me interesting, I have all the more reason to be myself.)

If it is troublesome to use the typewriter in a letter to me, don't. I can read your tentative script better than I can my own scrawls. I have no trouble reading the most difficult script. You figure it out by what ought to come next if by no other means. But an address is abstract, and may be anything, and usually is. In your case, I made it out Sute, but Suter makes no more sense, though I presume it is the name of a person that has been tacked onto a place. I filed some letters from you the other day, and read them again of course. And I found a copy of your *In Flanders Field*. Do you remember it? It was remarkably prophetic in your case and in the case of most of us who were at YHC at the time. I have often thought about all of us and how we were living with some zest and at times we were blithe enough under the thread-suspended sword. I remember we had a notion that war was coming but I don't believe we had much sense of its immediacy. I have been little affected by the war, but it is no fault of my own and, besides, I couldn't have known then that I would not also serve. I remember that in 1940 in that column I wrote in the county newspaper I offered to bet my bleached skeleton that we would be involved by a certain time (and we were) but even then I didn't believe it. It seemed impossible that the young fellows I know who were rather decent for all their small faults and without evil or hatred should be snapped up and cut off and without consulting their own will in the matter. The war was fought for a purpose certainly, and it has been won, but the peace hasn't been won. It will always be a matter of regret to me that I didn't go through the war and come out with a whole hide or at least with life. And therein is the catch. None of you had any assurance that you would come through with life. A lot of you didn't. Steve Hall didn't and any number you know didn't. You know, except for my own friends who were my friends before the war, I avoid soldiers. There has been so damned much tripe published about how to treat returned soldiers that there has been created a national phobia about it. I got a book to review for the *Journal,* called *The Long Road Home.* It is a remarkable and very good book, as far as its literary merit is concerned, but it adds fuel to the fire. It is by a participant and thus I am forced by reason to assume that the disease has penetrated to the soldiers too. As for me I try to treat those I am forced into contact with as human beings, and I must let it rest at that. So you see civilians have their problems too, and you brought this long tiresome speel upon yourself by writing that poem, which brought it up.

I have been hedging for about a thousand words now about the matter of Little Man [W. L. Dance]. If I had known that you didn't know he committed suicide, I don't suppose I would have told you. There are some who say that the only thing to do with facts is to face them, but I am willing to shunt them around if it makes me feel better. I don't believe though that you will be sorry that you found out when you have thought about it more. I have thought about him more since his death than I ever thought about him while he was alive. I have considered the matter from every angle and I have nothing to reproach him with. Not a single thing. I had been working late the Thursday I heard of his death. A neighbor boy is in school there, and he and his mother came by at dark and asked me to go to Young Harris with them. The boy who was very fond of little man wouldn't tell me that Prof. had shot himself. His mother told me. I didn't believe her, of course. But she insisted that it was true and the only thing I could say was "I'll be God damned." (If I am killed by any means that I was not suspecting, those will be the very last words I'll say, and I hope I won't be held guilty for them.) We went to YH and waited until midnight till the undertakers had prepared his body for burial. He looked utterly at peace and as if he were sleeping. I went to Atlanta the next morning early and didn't go to the service they held for him in the Chapel. He was buried at home in Eatonton.

He left a note to Sharp, and I have heard various versions of it. I think that he said he had been told by a doctor that he had cancer in the region of his sinus that would eventually reach his brain, and considered the means he was taking the best way out. I do not believe that was his reason. I have no grounds for that belief. It merely persists. Some think he was temporarily insane. He was no such thing. He attended a Lion's Club meeting the evening before he shot himself at two or three in the morning. No one suspected that he was not feeling as well as usual. You very well know that he had a cold analytical mind, and he would have thought the thing through and then he would have done whatever he considered best. He would have done it as he did it. Without hysterics or dramatics or fanfare. I don't know his reasons of course, but I respect and do not question them. I have admired him as much as any man I have ever known and his death at his own will has not lessened my admiration for him. I do not know where your obligation to those who love you ends, but as far as you yourself are concerned you have every right to kill yourself, if you reason the thing out and don't do the thing in a moment of passion or dejection when you would regret it immediately, were you not then beyond regret. Whether or not they commemorate his work at Young Harris, he has his own monument in the lives of many whom he has influenced and who loved him. He influenced me and I loved him.

I'll send on that photograph in a day or two. I meant to send you a study that flattered me. I have changed my mind. I'll send you a truthful study. I'm sending a review that appeared in the *New York Times.* I have already had two or three copies from friends. Well, for all I have been discussing I still feel good. But I have answered your letter in indecent haste so I'm going to chop this off here and have a cup of coffee and catch up on my cigarettes.

Faithfully,

Reece

BYRON HERBERT REECE
BLAIRSVILLE, GEORGIA

April 23, 1946

Dear G. B.

I having known you I can think of worse things than having you for a correspondent, not having you, for example.

I'll be in Atlanta the 29th, 30th and May first for the Book Fair. After that I'll have to stick to the farm come hell or high water until I get a crop planted. I'd like very much to see you, of course, and June also.

The photo I sent is not a very good one. It looks posed. I'll send you a better some time. I should have held out on you any way is order to induce you to –ee- (that last word is keep) reminding me to send it. In that way you would have to write something else too.

I'd be glad to have the clipping from the *Fort Valley Tribune*, if you can find it. I'll have a good bit of stuff in the Book Fair supplements of both Atlanta papers. I'll see if I can get some additional copies. By the way, I'll meet my publishers in Atlanta. So when they see me my goose may be cooked anyway.

This is a poor excuse for a letter but I am away behind with my correspondence. Let me advise you never to write a book. If it is at all successful it will work you to death. If it is not successful you will eat your heart out because it isn't. There's no escape.

I'm working on a long ballad I'll send you when it's finished, but it may be months before it's done.

If you are in Atlanta on the dates I mentioned you can reach me at the Hampton Hotel, which isn't far from Paramount. I've forgotten the street.

Faithfully,

Reece

BYRON HERBERT REECE
EDITORIAL REPRESENTATIVE FOR ALAN SWALLOW, PUBLISHER
BLAIRSVILLE, GEORGIA

August 6, 1946

Dear G. B.:

I'm trying to write this through the large sound of *Finlandia,* which strikes me as being the best piece of patriotic music ever written. One needn't be a native of any particular country to enjoy it, since "home is where the heart is." You and several other millions should know by now whether or not that is the truth. I finally broke down and bought myself a good portable radio for about what a second hand automobile used to cost. It hurts me to think of what I paid for it every time I turn it on.

Your long delay in answering my last letter reminds me that I hate to write letters very much myself. In fact were it not for the desperate need to keep contact with those who mean much to me I'd never write another one as long as I live. Does it ever strike you how very lonely people are, no matter how many friends they may have? Out of the long hours of the day one is contained within himself at least ninety-eight percent of the time. No one else knows what you are thinking or feeling, and on the other hand you don't know what another person is thinking or feeling no matter how close he or she may be to you.

I started this several days ago, so what I have written above must have been on my mind. I have been helping my brother haul acid wood and it takes all the sap out of me; nothing is on my mind at the moment … I feel almost as if I didn't have one. I've written only two or three poems within the last three or four months, nothing at all on my novel, and curiously I don't give a damn. I do write six or eight book reviews monthly, but that is merely a chore, it takes nothing creative from you. I don't like to review books, for one thing I am not honest about it. You know that I never cared to criticize the other guy's stuff at the QC meetings. If a book is terribly sorry it still took a lot of the author's time and his life blood to write it. I can't very well demolish all that labor in a snippy sentence or two … not that that would be likely no matter what I said about one for in the first place very few people read book reviews and in the second most who do have sense enough to disregard them.

I need to see you, I'm in a hell of a state with myself and I might be able to talk some of it out with you, but I'll have to wait till you get back to Georgia. I'm going to Atlanta to shoot a little bull to the writer's club there a week from Thursday. I was invited to speak to an audience in Columbus, but damned if I do. If I make any more appearances they'll have a hell of a price tag hooked to them. To ask abnormal rates is as good a refusal as any.

You may remember that when I wrote last we were having too much rain with the consequence that we had a time getting a crop planted. Now it is as much too dry as it was too wet then. If we don't have rain soon there'll be very little made in the fields in this neck of the woods. So, to break down the aura from the statement you liked, I fear God is falling down with His end of the business.

Here's a poem I wrote after I learned of Steve Hall's death. You might get a little something from it.

The spearmen, the bowmen, the archers
Move splendidly back of the brow;
When Steve was one with the marchers
I was alone with the plow.

Lonely among the boulders,
And bitter at heart, I turned
The earth while the press of shoulders
Moved toward the world that burned.

Still I go forth to the turning
Of earth, the generous loam,
But Steve to the world's burning
Went and will not come home.

Steve's dying ruined several musical pieces for me. I can't bear to listen to Beethoven's *First Symphony* nor Chopin's *Funeral March* among other things. He used to play both for me on the piano.

The clipping I'm sending will explain itself. The prospectus from Swallow will serve to remind you that you could probably write a good book, and if you would we'd see what could be done about it.

I hope you can find time to answer this. I frankly admit it isn't worth an effort on your part but I need a response from you anyway.

Faithfully,

Reece

BYRON HERBERT REECE
EDITORIAL REPRESENTATIVE FOR ALAN SWALLOW, PUBLISHER
BLAIRSVILLE, GEORGIA

January 2, 1947

Dear G.B.:

Thanks to you and June for the Christmas card. It's good to be remembered. Are you ever going to write to me again?

Faithfully,

Reece

BYRON HERBERT REECE
EDITORIAL REPRESENTATIVE FOR ALAN SWALLOW, PUBLISHER
BLAIRSVILLE, GEORGIA

April 2, 1947

Dear G.B.

I'm sorry that I've neglected your last letter so long, but I've scarcely been in the mood to write since the first of the year. You said you had the Mississippi misery, I suppose it's the Reece misery I have had lately. I can't account for the blue funk I've been in any other way.

Your 107 days in the Army should be well along toward expiration by now. I hope that when you get out we can get together if only briefly. I've need of a look at you.

Nothing of importance has come my way lately. I've done my usual stint of book reviewing for the *Journal,* had some poems in the new magazine published by the U. of Ga., *The Ga. Review.* I sold a poem to the *Sat Eve Post* a month or so ago, which puts me in the big league if only for once and that by a very brief poem and one I wouldn't think of reprinting in a volume. I deliberately slanted the thing for the post, and they took it, which should prove something or other, I don't know exactly what.

You as well as I must have been delighted by the decision of the Ga Supreme court declaring Hummon, as *Time Magazine* calls him, a pretender to the throne of Georgia. You won't have to settle in Miss. till 1948, when I'm afraid he'll come in by ballot.

I don't know what became of Prof's cabin. I haven't been on the campus of YHC since Little Man's death. I know I've never enjoyed myself as much anywhere as I used to when we would get together at the cabin for QC [Quill Club] meetings.

This is a poor excuse for a letter, but I wanted you to know I hadn't forgotten you. In fact I think I never shall.

My good regards to June.

Faithfully,

Reece

BYRON HERBERT REECE
EDITORIAL REPRESENTATIVE FOR ALAN SWALLOW, PUBLISHER
BLAIRSVILLE, GEORGIA

Sept. 1, 1947

Dear Mildred:

Sorry I couldn't make it over the weekend of P's birthdaying. I wanted to very much, but my youngest sister is at Battey, at Rome, in the hospital and some of us must drive over every weekend to see her. The weekend you wrote about was my turn. Even if I don't go myself the time is gone so I have no way to travel on weekends.

We have had a powerful dry spell in more ways than one. Six weeks ago I lost control of my nerves and folded up like a wet sock. With an immense effort of the will I'm able to stay out of bed and do a little wash. But I'm still on the verge of cracking up. I don't know how long I can play a tug-a-war with my nerves and I don't have the faintest notion, which will win.

I've finally got myself a fairly decent combination and a few good records. Why don't you and P. and the small fry run over sometime and see me? I hope everybody there's well. I hear through S. Daniel that Sue has betook himself in Guam. What goes [of] interest?

Faithfully,

Byron

BLAIRSVILLE, GA.

October 10, 1947

Dear Pratt:

An Army captain absconded with my copy of *Essay on Rime* over a year ago. If I go to Atlanta or some other large town soon I'll pick up a copy and send it to you. The burden of the whole thing is: The dead hand and exhaustion of our rime. It's more of a showpiece than anything else. In it Shapiro doesn't seem exhausted but there's more nonsense than sense in it. I looked into Lanier's *Science of English Verse* several years ago, when I was in school, and I don't remember having found much of value in it, though by reputation it is supposed to be one of the best things of its kind. I have not read Sartre, but I've read articles about him and reviews of his book in *Saturday Review*. I think he's barking up the wrong tree. I think he should stick to writing plays. They are good, by reputation again, I of course have seen none of them produced. I haven't even read them. I can't place Cox's *Indirections* at the moment though the title almost stirs a cord of memory.

I might explain here why I haven't written during the summer, and try to catch up with some of your letters. Early in July I suffered a nervous breakdown and for months I hadn't the physical or spiritual energy to do a thing in the world except go over and over again in my mind the events that led to my crack up. For a little over a month now I have been hard at work, physically and mentally. I've put up a lot of fodder and more hay, written a short story, revised a poetry volume mss and done dozens of book reviews. I am all right now.

I liked your "Summer Reverie in the Southland," and was glad to know it had been accepted by the *Southern Literary Messenger*. It has some of the strength of Thomas Wolfe in it. I hope you won't worry too much about form. Form is all right. I find it a necessary discipline, but if it comes hard and cramps you don't stick to any form. You can fashion your own. It seems to me from your letters and from the scraps of your work I've seen you could spend your time profitably writing a novel. Use your own life and perceptions. You have to have something to bind it into one piece, but you might think of where you came from and where, from the indications you can't have escaped noticing, you are going and work out a circle to contain the body of the large work. I don't suppose that is very clear but maybe you'll fathom what I mean by it. I liked "Wanted: Side Focus" in your letter of August 20th, too. How much stuff do you have that is in complete enough form to stand alone, such as the poem just mentioned? It might be we could work out something with The Swallow Press & William Morrow. Let me know about this.

It was hard not to tell you to come ahead when you mentioned visiting, but I was sick and my mother also. My mother is still ill. She is in bed most of each day and my sister who lives here teaches school and that throws me to have to do my own work and cook the midday meal in addition. I am still very busy; there is to be a highway change by our house and we are working like the devil to get things in shape. It involves moving our barn, crib and some other buildings. I hope your mother is better. You mentioned in one letter that she was in the hospital. A month or so later if you are not tied up with a job or school I'd like to have you come up for a week, say around Thanksgiving.

In one of the Western Reviews I sent there was a very fine poem by Conrad Aiken. I received it in book form for review else I would have been unwilling to part with that copy. The name of the poem was "The Kid." The passages printed in Italics are marvelous. I think there was a fine article on Franz Kafka in one of them. I don't remember whether I sent that copy or not. Kafka was undoubtedly a genius. I wish his works were more readily accessible in this country. I seem to remember you once expressed an interest in Kafka.

You mention Joe Drennan writing to you about Crane. I have never been able to work up too much enthusiasm about Crane. Some sections of his *Bridge* are as fine as anything done this century but his whole output is pretty ragged. Personally he was very ill adjusted. He was homosexually inclined, and that, I imagine, led as much as anything else to his suicide. If you ever have a chance read Philip Horton's biography of Crane. I don't know where you might find a copy as there is no large library near. As soon as I can find a copy somewhere, *Bones* has sold out to the last copy and none are available from the publisher. I want to send you a copy of *Bones* to pass on to Drennan. If I remember correctly you have a copy.

In a penned postscript to your last letter you note that "everything seems so useless sometimes." Certainly it does but believe me it isn't. I have been as close to death this summer as one can go and return again to life, and I haven't found one useless thing in the whole created universe. I discovered one thing by coming to the brink of death to do it. I am not selfish. If I had been I would not be writing this now. It is always easy to die. It is sometimes very hard to live. Once you have discovered this fast the hard way, living takes on a lot of new values and your eyes are opened to a lot of the old ones.

I'll send you a new batch of magazines in a week or so. If you should change your address let me know.

Faithfully,

Byron

BLAIRSVILLE, GA.

December 16, 1947

Dear Caroline [Greear]:

I wish I had a copy of *Bones* for you but I haven't a single copy except my own dog-eared and generally mis-used personal copy. I don't know where you might find one. It has sold out to the last copy. I ordered several copies two months ago and the publishers sent me two copies, the only ones remaining in their store rooms, and said they would alert their salesmen and tell them to pick up any copies that remained unsold in bookstores over the country which they would send to me if they had any luck that way. I have heard nothing from them since.

I haven't the faintest notion whether or not Dutton plans to reprint the book. Probably not before I publish a novel and so get my name before the public again. I haven't asked them. I have not wanted to call their attention in my direction lately, for I have a contract to deliver a novel and have already drawn advance royalty and until three weeks ago had done nothing about it for months. In the last three weeks I have written several thousand words and plan to have it done in rough draft by the end of March.

I was glad to hear from you again. I hope you are feeling stronger than when I saw you last. I hope to get over sometime during the holidays, but the chances are not too good. My sister who has been at Battey for the past few months is coming home on a furlough and it will be hard to get away from her. I suspect Philip and Mildred are not on speaking terms with me. I promised to visit them in Athens on a certain date and when that time came I was knee deep in concrete, casting a foundation for a barn we had to build to replace the old one that was in the way of the highway that's coming by and forgot that I had promised them to be in Athens on that day. Later I was so busy and felt so badly about telling them the story I didn't write and apologize.

I haven't heard from Sol. Thanks for his address. I'll write him this same night and maybe he'll get it by Christmas. Give my regards to Mr. Greear and to any of the others who may happen to be there.

Sincerely,

Byron

12/30/47

Dear Gaskin:

Thanks, first for the Sergeant, Kittridge English and Scottish Popular Ballads. It has already been useful in providing one version of the ballad I was looking for. I have also written a new ballad based on the situation of the Unquiet Grave. This is one of the most appealing short fragments in the language. It has haunted me ever since I read it in one of Prof. Dance's English books years and years ago. I don't however, accept the young man's weeping by the grave for a year and a day; hence this version of my own:

I'll do as much for my true-love (but integral paint of my V)
As any a young man may; (Stanza 2, Unquiet Grave)
I'll sit and mourn all at her grave
For a twelvemonth and a day.

But as he sat the grave beside
A day but barely one
He said, "It's hard to sit and grieve
While my hawk wings towards the sun."

But still he sat the grave beside
Where his true-love was lain;
O still he sat the grave beside
And his tears fell down like rain.

As he sat by the graveside
And wept upon the ground
He said, "It's hard to weep two days
And the fox before the hound."

But still he sat the grave beside
As he had sworn to do;
O still he sat the grave beside
And his tears fell down like dew.

As he sat by the graveside
Nor wiped his eyes at all
He said, "It's hard to weep three days
While my horse waits in the stall."

But still he sat the grave beside
Of her whom he had kissed;
O still he sat by the graveside
And his tears fell down like mist.

The fourth day by the graveside
The tears dried on his cheek.
He said, "I mind another maid
With whom I used to speak.

"It's hard to weep four long, long days
Beside a clay-cold form;
It's hard to love a clay-cold maid
While living maids are warm."

His first love in her clay-cold bower
He's left to take her rest;
He's plucked to him a second flower
To wear against his breast.

This is a first version, and I'll be happy to have any comment or suggestions for improvement. I don't know if it is anything more than a literary exercise, but it pleased me in the doing and that is the best way I have of judging if anything of my own is worth a damn.

Thanks for the comments and suggestions on the Fitz-James poem. I'll certainly incorporate three or four of the suggestions in the next version. You are quite right in your interpretation. The poem is a savage thrust of my own at-the-time-frustrated personality. I think however that the disguise will work with less knowledgeable people. After all it is carefully planned and executed on a second level. *The Midwestern Review* will print it this month some time. Would you like a published copy?

I think I may be serious about the opera on Mattie Groves. It will have to wait until the novel is finished but I'm going to have about two months free time after crops are laid by to work on the novel before deadline. I have already made Dutton practically disavow the deadline anyway. Nick Wreden, V.P. is one fine guy anyway. I'm glad I met him at the Book Fair in Atlanta. It gives me a wedge in the top drawers at Dutton. Vincent and I might turn out something popular in the way of opera, and if that should happen it could be very profitable. Folk stuff is on the upswing now as everybody who listens and looks knows. I think I can enlarge the fifteen or so versions of Mattie into a good long poem if nothing else. It's already perfectly plotted for three acts.

I failed to notice any impoliteness in the note, so can't accept any apology on that score. I may be overlooking something I should mention; but I have been harrowing all day, and that – I can't resist the temptation – is a narrowing experience.

Reece

BLAIRSVILLE, GA.

February 4, 1948

Dear Gaskin:

I told you that if it was at all possible I'd let you know two weeks beforehand whether or not I could make it down for the 14th. This will not quite reach you in the specified period but I thought it better to write you and let you know how things stand. There is one very good reason why I should come, and that is because I want to, but there are three or four reasons why I can't make it. The folks here have severe colds and I am finding it necessary to do the outside chores. Reason one. We have been having a well dug and water pumped into the house and have been to a good bit of expense and I find myself dead broke. Reason two. I think perhaps I shouldn't break into my writing habit now. I had to do so for three weeks around Christmas when my sister was on leave from Battey and she and her husband and daughter were here. I found it pure torture to make myself buckle down again. Despite the fact that a piece of work may be seeming to come along fine it goes more slowly than I for one had reason to suspect. That is to say that I have discovered that it takes a hell of a lot of words to make a novel. I hate like hell to miss the bull session with you – I make out all right about the music, I've got some new recordings and can hear three or four symphonies a week over WQXR, depending on the state of the weather. I believe you told me you could pick up somebody to keep from wasting a ticket. There is a vast difference between live and canned music, but I believe I enjoy the latter more in private than the former in public. It's very nearly impossible for me to keep still when I am listening to music. The first time I ever heard Haydn's 102 in B flat I lay down across the bed in the working gang house and bawled. That would be a rather embarrassing thing to do in public.

The novel still shapes up and I find I enjoy a lot of it though some of it comes like having teeth pulled. It will take me every day of the time left till deadline to finish it and get the Ms. in shape. I am going to write Dutton and tell them that my adventure with nerves in the summer set my schedule back by four months which it did in a way. But I'm going to put off doing that as long as I can. I need the sword of Damocles over my head to keep me at work.

I finished the long poem from Kings you read during the summer. I dressed out the rough spots and called it "Remembrance of Moab." (God said he would remember Moab for offering the son of the King of Edom as a burnt offering during the siege of Moab by Samaria, Judah and Edom. He remembered Moab by forsaking it.) It is out now to the *Land* though I doubt if they can use anything that long. It ran to sixteen double spaced pages in Ms. By the way, the *Land* is using the two Steve poems, with a program note, in the spring issue, and the whole thing will head off Country Voices department in the *Progressive Farmer* in the February issue. I'll get paid by both publications. I want to send Mrs. Hall a copy of both publications. Steve once told me her address is Ringgold, Ga. Route One. If you know any different I wish you would let me know.

I have written another ballad. Obscure deliberately, but outside of that it is one of the best I've done. When I get up the energy to type it for submission somewhere I'll send you a carbon copy. I also wrote a short story in November and have been letting it cool so I can tell whether or not it is worth the effort to type and submit. I'd like to have your opinion on it too and will send a copy some day. Of course I have to take brief vacations from the novel and I work on poems during those. I have a new Bible ballad, "John" that runs to spiritual rhythm, and is sort of in the answer-back song tradition. It goes like this;

Who is that in the wilderness?

John, John, John.

etc

I have done nothing notable or unnotable in the lyric lately. My feelings have not been compressed enough.

I kept thinking you would send me a follow-up of the summer story. Still what your letter suggested about study would be quite enough to keep the creative impulse buried, I imagine. What do the writers find in the air there? maybe I'd better come there and settle for awhile and see if I too can get rich.

Let me here from you when you have time and we must still plan to get together whenever it is possible.

Faithfully,

Reece

April 12, 1948

Dear Gaskin:

I am beginning to mistrust my ESP, or what-have-you, you are the third person from whom I have received communications while thinking about them. The other Saturday evening I suddenly went to the radio and turned on NBC and Toscanina and they were going into the marvelous first movement of Beethoven's Ninth Symphony which I wouldn't have missed for the world. That, incidentally, was a historic presentation. I am quite sure I have heard the greatest musical composition in the world conducted by the greatest conductor of Beethoven who has ever lived or is likely to. To further document my ESP, I have not been in the habit of listening to WQXR lately for various reasons. About two weeks ago I had an urge to try it, and they were playing Haydn's 102 B flat Major, which you have heard me rave about before. I don't suppose I am serious about all this but it does make you wonder at times.

Anyway, I was going to write you soon, so a letter from you was welcome, and would have been under any circumstance. My silence since February has been dictated by everything but labor on *Herbs.* My mother was seriously ill about that time, she had several hemorrhages, and continues ill but not dangerously so. Her illness added to the work I had been doing, physical and otherwise, almost set me back to my July adventure with nerves, but I decided, damn it all, that I simply couldn't afford a vacation in limbo, so I held on to them. The gain may or may not indicate I have gained control over my tendencies to fall to staves under difficult circumstances. I hope so. It is sort of a bad position to be in when you cannot absolutely trust your ability to hold on to yourself.

I'd very much like a session with you at Chapel Hill, or anywhere else, but I don't think I can make it during this quarter. A farm is the most despotic thing in the world in certain seasons of the year. We are inordinately behind due to extra work caused by the road construction and the wet weather. I'll be held mighty close till laying by time July. After that I am going to try to get free of the farm for a year or two. I simply must have some time now for my work. I'll never be in as good a position to amount to something again.

Besides staying so close and never having any conversation with others interested in the things I am, things get all out of focus. I am at times as cloddish as the Man with a Hoe looks. Whenever you can possibly manage it I wish you would come over for a spell and revive my creative interests. I badly need such a revival.

Herbs [Better a Dinner of Herbs] has stopped right now but I am beginning to get another movement of the story in focus and when it falls into place I think my interest will manage to shove things about so I can do another stretch of it. I will possibly finish it by deadline, but I won't have a clear copy for the publishers then, but that won't matter in particular. I think I'll go to Atlanta or somewhere when it is finished and hunt up a typist and have the thing typed. I hate typing when it is dead matter, just copying.

I think it would be a pity if your friend with the problem shouldn't be able to solve it. I myself have only one unfinished, I mean unpublished, but the unfinished applies too, since I have to polish it up, ballad right now. I had a good one but sent it off to the editor of the forthcoming *Midwestern Review* to be published by the University of Minnesota, the first issue coming from the presses in May. I'll enclose a carbon of that one, and ask you to return it because it is the only good copy I have left, and I'd hate like hell to have to reconstruct it from the original Mss. I wish you would make any suggestions for improvement that might occur to you. The editor of the *M R* asked for a poem for their first number. They might possibly not have space for the lengthy ballad I haven't heard from it yet. But to get back to the problem, I'll write your friend one if it will do him any good. I have two or three good ideas floating around in my head and one might jell under pressure. I am a great believer in oblique coercion. A young guy at the University of Minnesota, the editor I mentioned, might be able to help him too, since he is working on a collection of ballads and lyrics. The fellow's name is E.V. Griffith, who, if I remember correctly, started his poetic career off with a bang by selling a few lines to *This Week* magazine for two hundred dollars.

I have a request to make, since you are near a good library and I am not, could you secure me a copy of the old ballad "The Ballad of Mattie Groves"? It is #81 in the Child collection. I remember it vaguely but need to know, or have a copy of it. I am dickering with the associate professor of Music at University of Calif., John Vincent. He wants me to enlarge the "Mattie Groves Ballad" into a three-act opera libretto. I think perhaps I could do it, I think our tastes run in similar channels, though of course I'll have to know more in detail before I decide whether or not I want to take on the job.

A course in Shakespeare's tragedies sounds fine. It is a pity the instructor is uninspired. I will never, if I live to be a thousand, forget one line from *Lear,* which for money is the best Shakespeare. The line is

Thou'lt come no more,

Never, never, never, never, never. Pray you undo this button.

Thank you, Sir.

Nothing could be more moving than the conjunction of the most heart-rending cry and the utterly common-place everyday business of getting a button undone.

What in the name of God are you taking Greek for? Or is progress in it to be made with more speed than I have come to think. I thought it was a three or four year business to learn you way around in that language, but maybe you have studied Greek before. I come to consider myself more utterly unlearned everyday. By the way, the other day I burned down the editors of *Georgia Review* and recalled all my Mss. from them. They have had some of my poems two years without making a definite commitment to publish or not to publish. That is beating around the bush a little too long. Besides, I can't produce enough lately to supply those who care enough about my junk to invite submissions, not that those invitations come flying in every day, but I don't produce much either.

Sorry to hear of your Grandfather's death. I hope he was old and had accomplished whatever he had set out to do, much or little doesn't matter so long as it has been accomplished, or you have forgotten what it was that once fired you up when you were young and everything seemed possible. Sometimes death would catch me with a fistful of hopes and commitments, sometimes utterly empty handed I rather suspect though that if it were not for the valleys the mountains would not seem very high … and I also suspect I'm barely skirting sentimentality.

Faithfully,

Reece

P.S. It occurs to me that I am so wrapped up in my own creations I've misinterpreted the intentions of the guy wanting ballads. I suppose he isn't interested in contemporary literary ballads, but the old folk ballads. I have two or three such that I have never seen published, nor heard sung on any program or by any singer who specializes in such things. I have nothing really first class but if he's interested I'll be glad to let him know and see what I have.

The Heart and the Hand
Fitz-James

Fitz-James stood by his castle wall
As tall as a tree by his right hand stood,
And the lamp of day was beginning to fall,
As round and red as blood.

Fitz-James lifted his strong right hand
And caught the sun in his fingers four,
And it burned in his clutch like a flaming brand
And lighted up his door.

It lighted up his lintel low,
It lighted his door that was low and wide,
And through to the dark I saw her go,
His fair and fifth-month bride.

I saw his bride to the darkness go
And the door was shut, and Fitz-James stood
With the laggard sun in his right hand Oh
Where it burned as bright as blood.

And Fitz-James stretched his left hand out
And I beheld a marvelous thing,
Something his fingers were caged about,
And it began to sing.

"What is that cries, that cries with woe,
What is that cries in your strong left hand?
What is that cries in its strange cage O
I almost understand?"

"It is not a lark that sings so sad,
It is not a thrush that sings so wild,
It is not a mockingbird gone mad,
And it is not a child.

"It's not a wind that the leaf gives tongue,
Nor a brook the smooth stones orchestrate;
It is not a thing that has ever sung
Nor ever will, soon or late,

"Save here in my hand as I pluck its strings,
Save here as I pluck its strings apart,
Save here as I crush it because it sings;
It sings—and it is your heart!"

And I heard, and it was my heart that sang
In the cage of his hand like a lost thing.
It cried like a bird lost out of its nest,
It cried for its home in my empty breast.

And I cried to him who held my heart:
"How did you rifle my ribs apart
To take my heart from out of my breast
As a bird is stolen from out of its nest?"

And I cried: "Throw down, throw down the sun
And give my heart back into my side,
And turn to the face in the window wan,
O, go you in to your bride."

And Fitz-James opened his fingers four
And the sun from his opened fingers fell,
But my heart he crushed in his hand the more,
And it cried like a thing in hell.

My heart it cried, it cried in woe,
It cried in fear, it cried in rage,
It cried in the clutch of his left hand O
For the safety of its cage.

And Fitz-James cried: "When the trees to war
March forth, or the grass in the rolling tide
Of the seas take root will I restore
Your heart to your empty side!"

Then I said, "If he will not let you go
Turn in his hand a keen blade O,
And my heart heard me and obeyed
And turned in his hand a two-edged blade.

"If he will not free you as I desire
Turn in his hand a coal of fire."
And fire there burned in his left hand's cup
And the smell of his burning flesh rose up.

"If he will not free you for thrust nor burn
A nail and a nail for each hand turn,
And still for the finished deep provide
The spear that injures the crucified."

And my heart heard me and nailed the tall
Fitz-James fast to his castle wall,
And the spear that injures the crucified
Sank to its heft to wound his side.

Fitz-James hang from his castle wall;
The cry of his bridge from the darkness rang;
And he would fall but he might not fall,
From the nails of my heart he hang.

I laid my hand to my empty breast,
I fingered my aching side apart,
Like one that wheedles a child to rest
Did I call home my heart.

And the hanged one fell to earth by his door
As my heart flew home, a silent thing;
It will cage in the clutch of his hand no more,
And save in his clutch it may not sing.

And he lifted my heart in his hand and cried
"I did not thieve it from out of your side.
I looked to the winds and it was there,
I plucked it forth like a bird from the air.

"I did not thieve from your heart I vow,
I plucked it with apples that hand on a bough
I did not enter your side to loot,
I found it around the roses root.

"It was you heart, not I, to blame;
I did not take it but free it came
It came as a sparrow to pick a crumb
Held for its bill 'twixt my finger and thumb.

"Came as a cat in my warmth to bask,
Came as a dog a bone to ask;
Came as a pony to nuzzle my sweets,
Came as a beggar to taste of my sweets.

"Came as a stranger with me to dine.
Came for a visit and was not mine;
Came to be petted and fled from reach;
Came as a singer."

8-2-48

Dear Gaskin:

The NC polio didn't have me worried at all. I have been dimly aware that there was an epidemic there, I have read about it in the newspapers, I think, but never did connect it and my proposed visit. I assume of course that I am immune to everything I have not yet caught. The fact is, I am afraid to break into my writing routine right now. I am still going and have about got the whole thing blocked out. Another two weeks ought to do it and then I can let it cool before I approach it for revision, which, unless I am instructed by my publishers, will be minor, and concerned mostly with polishing of sentence, and probably a few additional sentences to clarify whatever might need clarification. This is not to say that the writing is at all inevitable, but there are millions of ways of doing a thing and if you don't settle on one of them you are lost. You could go on from now till the crack of doom doing variations of one theme. When I get the thing off my hands I will be happy whether it is a success or a flop or only middling. I had to do it, contract or no contract, to justify myself to myself because I had set my head on doing a novel. The next one I write, when and if, will be much better than *Herbs.* You learn a hell of a lot by doing a thing, and not one single iota about a thing by theorizing about it. The visit is not off, since you are good enough to understand my curious ways and habits, if I can squeeze it in between the completion of *Herbs* and fodder. If I shouldn't get to come down before then I'll come as early in the fall as possible after harvest. Since you don't hold me to my promises I don't hold you to a belief in them. You are free to doubt that I'll ever come, which you probably will. But I think you understand it is not because I lack the desire to do so. I can think of nothing I'd like better than a bull session and a few beers with you, and I know of nothing that would do me more good, but I am constantly bedeviled from all sides. My mother is still sick, and more mentally depressed about her health than the state of if warrants, but there is nothing we can seem to do to relieve her, so it all amounts to the same thing in the long run. I doubt if she will ever be up much again. My sister is teaching, and that leaves me with the midway meal to get, besides some other chores that fall to my lot. With the writing, and the press of the farm … we've simply got to dig our potatoes before they rot in the ground from the rainy weather, for example, I am run ragged. And my temper shows it. The other day I burned Angus Perkerson's chin whiskers off because he hadn't run some articles of mine he had been holding a long time. He deserved it, of course, but I never would have blasted him so completely, I have a horrible facility for demolishing people, if my nerves hadn't been stretched out of order. The old buzzard was badly hurt at me, and I rather liked the fact that he was, which is, I suppose a bad symptom of something or other. I'll let you know a few days beforehand if I can come down.

Once you wrote me something or other about somebody whose only contact with me had been "Ballad of the Bride and Groom" before you introduced him to *Bones,* and asked if I had a copy. I haven't a printed copy but I'm sending a revised typed copy, not the ultimate revision, I think, but its better. If he or she or whoever it was is still around you can give them this copy. I have written nothing since the Unquiet Grave take-off. Incidentally I appreciated your comments on that. And as for the hawk wheels toward the sun the hawk was one of the knight's or gentleman's trilogy in those days as you probably know. I have a beauty in mind from one of child's descriptions of a Scandina.

8-30-48

Dear Pratt:

Thanks for your letter. I have been meaning to write for a long while, but I remain always pressed for time. Lately I have been at work on my novel, *A Dinner of Herbs,* in case I haven't told you the title before, which I think I have. I have written three or four people about it lately and I get mixed up about it. At any rate the title comes from Proverbs, 15th ch., 17th verse, or the reverse, Better is a dinner of Herbs where love is than a stalled ox and Wrath therewith. The captitals, I think, are mine. I may be proving my text in reverse, but that is as good a way as any. I think perhaps the title will stand, publishers are notorious title changers; I turned in a fourth of the Mss. a couple of weeks ago and they seem to be tremendously impressed by the writing. That is rather heartening, for a publisher is the last person in the world to admit the quality of a piece of work. However, there remain the hurdles of the remaining three quarters of the book. The second quarter is done in rough draft and the rest, partly blocked out is writing and partly in my mind. Harvest is coming up and I'll have to take out time for that, despite the fact that the first of September is my deadline. I am happy that deadlines are usually pretty flexible; nevertheless I get pretty well frustrated between writing and farming. The two do not go well together, whatever you may hear to the contrary. Both make too many demands on your energy and time.

Your last letter or two interested me greatly. I wish I could have answered them immediately. You remember writing to me about *Other Voices, Other Rooms,* and objecting to the photograph of Truman Capote. What I have been trying to establish is why men reacted as they did to the photograph (No women objected publicly at least.) Is Capote's pose seductive? After seeing Paul Strahl's comment in *Saturday Review,* and Merle Miller's reported in *Time* I wrote a Jingle for the *Saturday Review,* which they said they were publishing in the letters to the editor, but never did. The jingle went like this to the best of my memory:

Since Strahl's impelled to make attack
Because Capote is on his back,
And Millar thinks that he should hang
Because he doesn't like his bang,
The two perforce must think <u>me</u> mad:
I think Capote's a handsome lad,
And cannot fathom what his looks
Have got to do with writing books.

That's my general attitude about the whole matter, which was in no way important but rather interesting. Anyway, the whole thing panned out for Capote pretty well. The last time I heard his book was selling at the rate of 3600 copies a week.

The coming season would be wonderful if one had time to enjoy it. Nothing appeals to me as much as the color in autumn hedges. The autumn landscapes here positively undo me at times. I get the same reaction to them as to great music. It hurts me tremendously that I have yet failed to capture any of it in writing. There is no way of doing it, or at least I have discovered none. I am hurt also at the passing of time, at no time more apparent than in autumn. That last is a poor sentence. But I think you will get what I mean. Do you ever think suddenly, perhaps from deep enjoyment, God, this day is gone, this hour is gone, and neither will ever come again? I have long had in my mind the intention to write a Ballad of Things Finished. I hope I get around to it some of these days.

Thanks fore noting the reprinting of "Gathers Again to Shining." My copy of *PF* hasn't arrived yet. I'll have a poem in the Autumn *Land,* and a few others scattered about here and there. I write little verse these days. I mean to get back at it as soon as the novel is finally approved by the publishers and I can forget it.

This is not all I meant to write, but it will have to serve. I am drunk with lack of sleep. Last week I lost several nights' sleep altogether, in staying with one of my Uncles whose son, my favorite cousin and my own age, died with a heart attack.

Let me hear from you.

Byron

[Autumn 1948]

Dear Gaskin:

It would seem that I could have gotten over as far as Chickamauga, but the fact is that I'm in the middle of fodder season and work all day and sometimes far into the night taking up the cured blades. I did so last Saturday and felt altogether too pooped out to do anything. By the time I had driven over Sunday I couldn't have stayed more than an hour or so. So it seemed best to put off the visit till a later time when I won't be so rushed.

Since I wrote last I turned in the first section of *Herbs* to Dutton. They approved it and that is that. The rest is roughly blocked out, but I am going to have to do a hell of a lot of knocking it into shape. It will probably take me two months to put it together to suit myself. I find anything that sort of suits me stands up pretty well in the trial by market everything must come to, to quote Frost. Wreden, my contact at Dutton's, says of the first part of *Herbs,* "the writing is perceptive sensitive and beautiful, the section turned in has a completeness and perfection about it that should afford you a tremendous satisfaction," and he adds that he can see why I can't see so objectively at this time. Wreden has since left for Europe and will not be back before November 8, so if I have the second section ready by that time I'll be all right. And of course I'll have it done if nothing out of the ordinary turns up. I expect to turn in the whole thing in time to have the load off my mind by Christmas so I can celebrate in true Xmas spirit. Not a word from Wreden, V. P., nor Macrae, P., about the deadline which was passed a couple of weeks ago.

Thanks for the commentary on "Ballad of the Bride and Groom." Your suggestions make it a much stronger poem. I'll retype it and send you a copy as soon as I have time.

I pass another little time post tomorrow, which bothers me a little, for I am not nearly as young as I used to be, and at the rate I complete projects I'll have to live to be very old to accomplish much.

The University of Kentucky business would be worth looking into. They have some pretty sound intellectual timber there. Besides I think I'd like the region.

So much for now,

Reece

BLAIRSVILLE, GA.

Day after Christmas [1948]

Dear Gaskin:

I meant, as usual, to write you long before but, or usual again, I didn't get around to doing so. You are one of the few people I can write in script, (at least you have never said you couldn't read my handwriting) and that gives me a little vacation away from my typewriter. I'm having to use it altogether too much lately. One of the reasons I have not written sooner should please you - I have been working furiously on *Dinner of Herbs* when I was not moving barns, gathering corn, and so on. I wrote about 15 thousand words or the whole 1st section in about 2 weeks. That will run to 17 thousand words when I have worked it over again. There are two more sections to come yet, and I am afraid the book will run to more words than I had at first intended. I have some unrelated chapters completed on each of the other sections and if nothing comes up to keep me from working on it, I should finish the 1st draft by the last of March. It will take me part of the summer to rewrite I have to so that slowly; else I'll rewrite the life out of a piece of work. I'm really enjoying writing the thing now that I have got started, and I mean to make a good job of it if I'm capable, because I have no intention of working that much time and effort if I can help it; mind it will be a little startling, perhaps, a little hard to read but worth the effort for those who care about conceptions.

But let's not get too enthusiastic about it yet for it's a long ways out of the words still.

I think perhaps I can make it for the week-end when the Philadelphia Orchestra will be in Raleigh. But we won't make it definite yet. You never can tell what will come up. I'll let you know for sure-if such a thing is possible-2 weeks before the actual date.

"The Lord" finally sent me a check for $20 for "now that the apple trees are bare." I have sent the editor two other poems for the winter mo., by invitation. I have little time to send out stuff and usually do so only on invitation these days. I am about up with my output at that. By the way, I notice a former Ga. boy, Fitz-Simmon, of the U. of N. C. has sold movie rights to an unfinished novel for $75 thousand. He teaches drama or some such at Chapel Hill.

Had a Christmas card from Miss Jane at Rome, does she live there? I'm in Rome from 2 to 3 times a month. If I know her address I'd try to find her sometime when I'm there.

Among my Christmas acquisitions is an album of Ruben Stein playing Roehmaninoff's Concerto No. 2 in C. minor. I have heard a lot of good music lately, new recording of B's [Beethoven's] 9th but it is a part war recording and the surfaces are bad. I wish I had a pre-war victor recording of all B's symphonies. I have come to like his 7 or more or any of them.

I think this will furnish you enough mental exercise for a bit.

Faithfully,

Reece

Seem I forgot to mail this.

R

12/31/48

Dear Pratt:

I was beginning to think that you were perhaps overwhelmed in love and had deserted me. Thanks for the copy of *Albron Moonlight,* which I am happy to add to my library. I think Patchen is a very extraordinary failure. I have read a good deal of Patchen poetry but this is the first prose of his I have read except for the first short story of his published, that was many years ago in *Household Magazine,* and an installment or so of a conventional novel of his in *Woman's Home Companion* recently. I have even forgotten what the title of the *WHC* novel was. It was as slick and without value as any of the loner things that appear in *Woman's Home Companion. Albron Moonlight* is certainly an odd book and a powerful one; nevertheless I think it is a failure. The conditions of art are not the conditions of chaos. As a matter of fact the whole aim of art, and of life itself, is to unify, to integrate the haphazards of circumstance. Patchen threw away his chance to write a magnificent symbolic fantasy. You will see now he could have done it if you remember his first descriptions of Rovias; now he was known by all sorts of names but could be identified by the fact that his little finger was missing. Then, a few pages later, Albron Moonlight remarks about rubbing the place where his own little finger was missing. Thus he identifies himself as Rovias, which one suspected all the time. After that, though, the symbolism of the journey even blows up and the latter part of the book, which is sometimes magnificent in itself, is hopelessly at loose ends with the rest of the material. The book as a whole is not equal to the sum of its parts, and this is the more disconcerting because Patchen wrote it that way with an intense deliberation. Patchen is probably sexually impotent; the numberless sexual episodes in the book, without purpose so far as I can see, moved me to say with Bill S. Methinks the lady doth protest too much. On the other hand, he may be over-sexed. It is none of my business and I don't care so long as he confines his sexual activity to his private life and quits thrusting it on his readers. I prefer Patchen's kind of failure to most of our popular successes, and his sexiness is sometimes obviously a parody of the big-bosomed historical romances, as in other instances his writing about soldiers is a parody of the war literature of the Passos-Hemingway generation. What really irks me is that a man of Patchen's talent should squander it. This judgment of course merely reflects my own opinion concerning the purpose of art, and despite his protestations his work must be considered an art, but I think my opinion is sounder than his practice.

I'm glad you liked "Roads" in the *Land.* I enjoyed your poem anew in the *Land.* I hope you will cultivate Lord and the *Land.* It is important that the writer write and nothing will spur you along as much as having your work appear in good places. I have not yet finished *Herbs,* and I have got to the place where I have given up thinking of it as finished. I merely work on it as the urge moves in me. I can write nothing dead, that is if I feel nothing to say I can't force myself to write so many dead words. *Herbs* will also be a failure of a sort, but not a personal failure. I am saying as nearly exactly what I want to say as it can be done. I think I have already remarked to you about the gulf that exists between the inspiration and the execution of any work.

Let me hear from you as you find time. I am more pressed for time than ever. I have been invited to appear at the University of Georgia for a couple of days next month. I will do one public lecture and reading and meet a couple of classes. I'll have to spend some time getting the material I will use in some sort of order, though I usually speak out of my head (in more ways than one, some think).

Faithfully,

Byron

BLAIRSVILLE, GA.

27 January 1949

Dear Gaskin:

As I have probably told you before I have a text (in the sense that a preacher has one) for everything, and the one in my mind right now comes from Yeats, I think, though I wouldn't swear it.

But time runs on, she said;
Come, out of charity,
And dance with me
In Ireland.

Now of course the last three lines have nothing to do with the case, but the mind likes to have a little completeness though part of what constitutes the completeness runs beside the point.

At any rate it has been a long time since I have written you, but like Miniver I have reasons. They are all pretty good ones too but I won't bother you with listing them.

In the meantime, I got together a collection of ballads, five or six, I have forgotten now, and submitted them in *American Weave's* publication award contest, just for the hell of it, and I won. The award is just a little hard to discover, it being merely publication of the brochure on a royalty basis, with-ten free copies and thirty percent royalty on 300 copies at fifty cents each. Well, anyway it gave me a chance to publish one or two I don't want to publish in a full collection, such as "Ballad of the Lost Shoes" perhaps, and possibly three others in the collection. Three reserved the right to reprint them at will from the brochure, which is called a *Remembrance of Moab,* and which will be published sometime between now and next fall, at the publisher's leisure, I presume. Those three are the title poem, "Ballad of the Bride and Groom," which has turned, with your aid, into a respectable poem, and "I'll Do As Much For My True Love." Mr. Williams, the publisher and editor of *American Weave,* is eminently respectable and is connected each summer with the Bread Loaf Writers Conference. The brochure will bear a dedication to you, unless you forbid it, and I'll see that you get copies as soon as it appears. I adapted your version of the next to the last couplet in "Bride and Groom" to:

Of Silent brides and grooms who meet
Loveless in death's cold bridal suite.

Which is pretty chilly. (You may not remember how that goes and then this won't make sense, but the trouble is I don't remember exactly what comes before that either, and I am too lazy right now to look it up.)

Incidentally I had Dutton's permission to print those poems, else I would not have submitted them to another publisher. I mean to submit a full collection of lyrics in *Poetry Awards'* contest to be held next summer. The prizes are a first of one thousand and a second of five hundred dollars with no strings attached. *Poetry Awards* will distribute $3500 among poets of the English speaking world this year and during the next two. Then the good Samaritan who foots the bills, whoever he is, will decide whether or not he thinks the poets are worthy of that much money on a yearly basis. Funds are already guaranteed to continue if the committee, who will help decide if the project will continue, is worthwhile. On the committee are several friends of my work, including Dutton's poetry editor, Louise Townsend Nicholl, Robert Hillyer, Robert Nathan, who wrote a nice press release for *Bones* that was never published, and John Hall Wheelock.

A Dinner of Herbs comes on apace. Half of it stands approved; at least the first section has been approved and highly praised. The second part stands approved to the extent that I have been paid for it (I have not had a report). (Wrenden has not been back from Europe long and I assume he is snowed under with work that piled up in his absence, and he has taken me on as his personal responsibility). The third quarter went off today, and I anticipate unconditional approval of it, for it contains some of the best work in the whole thing. The fourth quarter is practically complete. I lack gathering up the edges and making a good copy, which will take me a couple of weeks when I settle down to it. I am taking a few days mental vacation on the completion of the third quarter. My wordage stands at approximately 54,900 words with the completion of the three quarters.

My time is still filled to overflowing. I have purchased, with my brother, a tractor, and we have practically mortgaged our souls to pay for it. I dare not waste a minute of workable weather, and it has been lovely here of late, all winter, in fact. In April I am going to spend two days on the campus of the U. of Ga. I will speak and read at an open meeting, probably chapel; this I don't mind and it will not cause me extra work because I have already built up a backlog of bull for that sort of thing. But I will also meet with a poetry class, a journalism class, and a graduate class in English, besides two social functions, one a dinner with the English faculty and the other a tea with special students. I will have to prepare material for the three classes, having had no occasion before to prepare material for the three classes, having had no occasion before to prepare material for that sort of thing. The fee will be a hundred dollars, which is not much for so much work, but since I need money so badly and can make that much to close to home I thought I had better not turn down the opportunity. Besides the contacts may be worth something. Let me hear what you are up to when you find time.

Faithfully,
Reece

P.S. Notice your boy Graham is under considerable fire these days.

BLAIRSVILLE, GA.

18 March 1949

Dear Gaskin:

For all the madness of your scheme I would take you up on it except for two facts: My sister has to drive the Jeep every day in the week except Saturday. She can't very well walk eight miles. And I am committed to a Tea, as an honored guest, in Atlanta on this weekend. The Tea is even madder than your scheme and I hardly know how I got involved in such a thing. It is to benefit the Pearl Henry Foundation, of which you would naturally know nothing, and the P. H. Foundation is to benefit children in an out of the way section of this county, in the general neighborhood of where I used to teach school, and I suppose it is this fact that led me to accept their invitation.

I dearly hate to disappoint you once more, but there is nothing else for it. My sister's school is out on the 29th of April, and I shall after that drop down for a weekend, or up, whichever it is. True, there may not be as much room and quiet as on the forth-coming weekend, but I can put up at an hotel if necessary, for by then Dutton will have paid me for the remaining half of my novel, I hope.

As for the novel, I finished it on February the eleventh, henceforth a red-letter day for me, and sent it in to Dutton. Until this day I have had nary a word from them, except to acknowledge receipt of the Mss. The first half passed muster all right, and I hope the remainder does so too without having to rewrite any appreciable amount. As a matter of fact, I wrote all I intended to write, have forgotten the whole thing; it is out of my system and if they want any major revision I fear they will be out of luck. I shall send it to the two other publishers that want a look at it. The novel is all of a piece, and I don't think I wasted my time writing it.

I have also prepared a poetry manuscript for the contest I spoke of earlier, severely selected and limited to forty-two poems. And since finishing the novel I have written a slew of new ones, lyrics, sonnets and ballads. When I am firmly in control of the ballad, but the lyric is something else again. I sometimes find mine settling out of control like a fallen cake. I am beginning to publish poetry here and yan again, by invitation and otherwise. It amuses me that *The Lyric,* the second oldest poetry mag in existence, that used to reject me regularly has asked for contributions. I am at work on a ballad of protest "A Ballad of Robert Mallard." Nough said.

Faithfully,

Reece

Your letter arrived on the 17th which was three days from date; mine will probably not reach you.

BLAIRSVILLE, GA.

29 March 1949

Dear Pratt:

I have taken advantage of your admonition not to write letters to you if I was at work on something else. I enjoyed your letter of February 4; it seems almost impossible that it was that long ago that it arrived. I liked the "Constant One" in the *Yogi's Self Realization Magazine,* and "The Look Toward Spring," And Thanks in your letter. The two poems seem pretty closely related, in treatment and subject matter. It seems to me that you shouldn't have a great deal of trouble placing your poems, as perhaps you don't.

What I started out to say in the first paragraph: I finished *A Dinner of Herbs* on the 11th of Feb. I just yesterday got Dutton's final report on it. It was accepted, "with enthusiasm and much feeling" to quote the Vice-President in charge of manuscripts. I am happy that it was accepted as written, not a word is to be changed, unless I take a notion to alter a few sentences myself in galley. It will be published next January. It could not possibly be produced before October, and that is a bad time for me, for I am always busy at that time with harvest, etc. At the tail end of the year the critics are worn out and trying to get caught up with the year's crop of books. So January seems the best time for it to appear. I have worked on it so long that the delay in its reaching print doesn't bother me at all. I am rather glad to be free of the burden of autographing and allied activities the publication of a book forces on one for a few months. I feel impelled now to do nothing at all, so what I do accomplish, if anything, I can enjoy. Do it for its own sake. I'll probably sign a contract for a second novel this fall, if Dutton approves the theme I have been sort of considering in my head. I'll have a brochure out sometime during the summer. I won *American Weave's* publication award for 1949. Did I tell you? I'll send you a copy when it comes out.

Well, I got off the track again. After finishing the novel I had a batch of ideas for poems in my head and I have been working on them steadily since the novel was finished. I have written fifteen or twenty sonnets, perhaps more. Five or six lyrics, one or two good ones, worked on a long ballad-like narrative of David and Jonathan. I will probably not publish it, though some of it is very good dramatic writing. I think I shall submit a section, The Crows at the Parting of David and Jonathan, to Neurotica, and it will probably fold, if not already, before I get around to fulfilling my intentions. I don't think I can explain my reluctance to publish the thing as a whole unless you had read the ms. And I'll probably conquer my reluctance anyway if the whole thing turns out to be any good. My treatment of their relationship stems to a certain extent from the book *David the King* wherein the two were in love, not a strange thing in Canaan in those days, but frowned upon in Israel, but I had the thing in mind before Miss Schmitt's book came out. This came from my reading of Old Testament books of Samuel, Judges, Kings, etc, and scholarly books of the period. All the critics commented on the beauty of the relationship of D. and J. in Miss Schmitt's book. Very well then. But their relationship was Freudian all the same, a homosexual attachment, which is a different matter from saying their relationship was that of perverts, since the former phrase indicates only the direction of the id. Besides this, I have been working on a ballad of protest called "A Ballad of Robert Mallard." If you followed his story in the newspapers the title will explain the ballad. I intent to let *Life's* editors have a look at it as soon as I have time to make a good copy of it. They published pictures of the trial where two white men were accused and acquitted of his murder. His widow became hysterical at the trial and wept, and men in the courtroom snickered at her grief. When I read that I was thoroughly and truly ashamed that I was a member of the human race and wanted to ask every dog's pardon I met for days afterwards.

I think you asked if we had gum trees here. We have both sweet and black gums, and if there are other varieties I do not know about them. The sweet gums are most beautiful in the fall of the year, having the richest color of any tree as its leaves change.

I enclosed a page from the winter *Land* with two sonnets. I have since rewritten the first of the two and shall probably rewrite the second sometime. I'll have a couple of poems, a sonnet and a lyric in the Spring *Land*. I also entered *P. Farmer's* winter singing contest, just for the hell of it. There was only twenty dollars to gain and nothing to lose. The *Lyric* of Roanoke used to reject my poems regularly. Lately I have sent them poems at their request, which they were glad to accept, and they asked for more later. It amuses me that the quality of my work has changed with the growth of my reputation. I am reminded of Housman's "When first my way to fair I took". I hope you remember that poem. I hope you remember all of Housman.

And I hope you will forgive my delay in answering your letter and will write when you have time.

Byron

BLAIRSVILLE, GA.

30 March 1949

Dear G. B.:

All your laziness to the contrary, I assume you will be interested to know that I have given birth to another brain child (and if actual birth is any harder to live through I bless the Lord for my maleness). There's no rush about telling the news, but I have been so long at work on it that now it is off my hands I feel like shouting. My novel *A Dinner of Herbs* has been finally approved by Dutton and will be published next January. By that time you ought to be able to work up enough energy to congratulate me. I am just a bit puffed up over the fact that the editors did not even want to monkey with my text, which is a most extraordinary circumstance. One of them has called my novel a perfect piece of narration, done with unflagging skill and consistency. I take that with a grain of salt but it is good for my ego, especially after the trials I went through writing the damn thing. Brother, never write a novel. (I'm mulling over an idea for a second one right now.)

Couldn't you wander up this way again on some pretext or other? I'd dearly love to behold your mug again. I have almost forgotten what you look like. My friends have all become so muchly married and domestic I feel lost and left out. Philip Greear is a staid farmer-father these days, even Leon Radway is married and I presume settled down. I haven't seen him in a year or so.

Now that the novel is out of the way I am going to write a libretto for an opera, in collaboration with John Vincent of the University of California who will do the score. I have written a slew of new poems since finishing the novel, but I find I fare pretty poorly in periodical publication. I have got so I rarely submit anything to the magazines. I farm to eat. I can wait on book publication. There at least I have been luckier than any young writer has the right to hope.

My best to June.

Faithfully,

Reece

April 8, 1949

Dear Pratt:

I've been too busy to breathe for the last three or four weeks, (put in 15 ½ hours last Thurs., 13 Friday, etc.) and that's why I have neglected your letter and am just now thanking you for the copy sale. Thanks for sending it along. I like "Scenanio," but less than the others poems you have showed me lately. I'll try to subscribe soon.

Normally I receive one copy of the *Land* as soon as it comes from the press (as a member of Friends of the *Land*) and anywhere from a week to a month later two contributions copies. The laxity sometimes evident is due to the business office, which being non-profit is probably under-staffed. I have never had dealings with more considerate, courteous people than Land and his staff, also the officers of Friends of the *Land* itself are wonderful people.

My visit to the campus of Univ. of GA. was postponed once again, and I go there the 17th & 18th. Back home then to try to finish my planting. On the 26th I'm scheduled to speak at the banquet meeting of the Writer's Club in Atlanta. From June 7 to 10 I'll attend the Second GA. Writer's Conference at Emory-at-Oxford, appear on a round-table discussion, etc. I hope to have the rest of June free to take care of my cultivating. I'm becoming entirely too involved in extra-curricular activity for my physical good. With all the physical labor I do the additional strain of all this speaking and gallivanting around begins to be too much. It is unfortunate that a writer is not allowed to write without all this other activity imposed on him.

It is entirely reasonable for you to use the title "Mountain Thought-etc." Incidentally this is one of your very fine poems.

I am stuck on the Jonathan-David piece, right now, due, I think, to my inability to decide if it is worth doing as conceived. I'll try to send you a copy of it as far as it has progressed before very long. I am beginning to share the attitude of one of Housman's characters in the poem beginning: "I promise nothing."

Besides other worries and work, our Bank at Blairsville failed two weeks ago, which left me flat broke, and several responsibilities to meet again, since checks I had recently given bounced at the Clearing House.

But, as an old woman says in one of Jame Still's short stories, I guess "I'll endure."

Faithfully,

Byron

BLAIRSVILLE, GA

23 May 1949

Dear G.B.

It ain't a cash book, though it certainly is a concoction of strange ingredients. In the book of Proverbs is a saying, which goes like this: Better is a dinner of herbs where love is than a stalled (or fathered) ax and wrath therewith. So it is about love, Sacred and propose. More than that I can't tell you with out using as many words as it took to write the book. You'll just have to wait and see. It won't seem long. See, it's been a couple of months since I first mentioned it or has it? I forget.

Spoke to a bunch of jack-asses at the University t'other day. The more I see of academic life the happier I am to have none of it. Hope you and June can get up this way later in the summer.

Love,

Reece

Lyrics for Sing Holly-loo

1. Christ Jesus had three gifts from men, all in the stable where He lay, from Wise Men seeking grace to win, at Bethlehem on Christmas Day, Oh, sing holly loo, sing holly-loo Christmas Day.

2. The first gift was a gift of gold, all in the stable where He lay, to buy Him garments against the cold, at Bethlehem on Christmas Day, Oh, sing holly-loo!

3. "The Christ Child has a lovely face," all in the stable where He lay, said one, and he was clothed with grace, at Bethlehem on Christmas Day, Oh, sing holly-loo!

4. The next gift was an odor sweet, all in the stable where He lay, Him to anoint from head to feet, at Bethlehem on Christmas Day, Oh, sing holly-loo!

5. "The Christ Child He is fair of limb," all in the stable where He lay, said one, and grace came over him, at Bethlehem on Christmas Day, Oh, sing holly-loo!

6. The next gift was a rare perfume, all in the stable where He lay, that wise men dreamed of Joseph's tomb, at Bethlehem on Christmas Day, Oh, sing holly-loo!

7. "Then, Wise Man, grace abide with thee," all in the stable where He lay, Redemption shall my one gift be, at Bethlehem on Christmas Day, Oh, sing holly-loo!

Around Oct. 29, 1949

Dear Pratt:

Thanks for your letter and the poems. I am much impressed by the poems and I have a suggestion to make about them. Bundle up some of you best ones, say sixty-four in number, and send them to Mr. Herbert Weinstock, Executive Editor, Alfred A Knopf, Inc., New York. (I'll send the Street address later, I have forgotten it). Say to Mr. Weinstock that I asked you to send the poems to him. That I said he was the sort of editor to counsel and encourage a young, vital poet. Mr. Weinstock wrote me not long ago wanting to see my novel. He did not know that it had been underwritten by Dutton. I believe he is the man to see your poems. I know Knopf is one of the most progressive publishers in the business and if ever I desert Dutton I am going to Knopf first.

I should have written you during the summer, but I did a lot of things, had little time and was sort of drifting on a sense of ease and well-being, it being the first time in years I had nothing compelling to do except carry on the work of the farm. Now I have signed a contract for a second novel, *Tents Toward Sodom,* and there are a thousand things to which I am committed and life becomes a bed of nettles again until all my responsibilities are discharged. Now I have received an invitation from the English Department of the University of California to conduct a course in verse writing, and a course in the short story in summer school there next year. The offer is too tempting to turn down, the opportunity to go to California, the opportunity to discharge a job I think I can do, (though it will take a hell of a lot of work preparing) and they offer twelve hundred dollars for an hour and forty minutes each school day from June 19 to August 11.

Of course I will send you a copy of the Autumn *Land* as soon as copies reach me. They are reprinting a section from the novel, called "The Time of the High Sun." It touches a bit on one of the relationships explored in the novel. Lord liked it a lot. Of course the excerpt is not complete, and takes up the relationship far over in its progress, but I think it suggests the whole relationship and is fairly compelling within itself. I'll send you a copy of the complete novel as soon as it is published which will be in January, the exact day has not been announced. It has already been catalogued and the catalog sent out to book buyers all over the country. I have had word from some of the bookstores in Georgia saying they have already ordered for stock. Naturally I hope it sells well, for I am in need of the money it is possible for it to bring in. I am still writing poems now and then. One I recently sold to *Southern Fireside,* a new magazine published in Birmingham for a hundred dollars. I had a poem in the first issue of *SF* and it was set to music by a composer in Birmingham.

I don't know it he will find a publisher for the music. It doesn't matter to me greatly. The poem was "John, A New Testament Ballad," and I am adapting it for a Negro Spiritual. One of my recent poems, "The Gifts," a Christmas poem that will appear in *Southern Fireside,* has been set to music by John Vincent of the music department of the University of California. He is practically certain of finding a publisher. He has had many musical works published and we are to do an opera together finally, as I have probably told you before. Why don't you try *Southern Fireside* with something? The address is 215 Exchange Building, Birmingham 3, Alabama. They are interested in encouraging the poets of the South. Say that you are from the South and that I suggested you send something to them.

What of the school you are attending? Do you like the West? It seems to me that I would enjoy it immensely. It is still God's earth, too wide and big to be cluttered much with the works of man. I hope sometime to live part of the year around Santa Fe. Have your tried the *Land* with "Of Some of the Created Things," etc.?

I think Bernard Raymond is right about the New Criticism. (I'm glad you have made contact with him, for he seems to me intelligent and interesting.) If you care to read the new criticism by all means read Yvor Winters. His *In Defense of Reason* is by all odds the best of the new criticism. You will probably find it in the library there. My advice is to ignore the criticisms old and new and never think of them when you are writing. Your job is to write, the critics' job is to criticize after you have written. I think it is utterly confusing to try to fulfill the tenets of some school of criticism while in the middle of a creative work. That is what is wrong with a lot of "modern" verse. The writers are all sicklied oe'r [with] the pale cast of Eliot.

My good wishes as always, and try to write that long letter before too long.

Faithfully,

Byron

BLAIRSVILLE, GA.

December 1, 1949

Dear Gaskin:

It was good to have your letter. I was wondering if you weren't snowed under with work. I can understand that. A couple of weeks ago I sent you a copy of *Moab,* but since I didn't have any other address I simply sent it to you at the Univ. of N.C. It will probably filter down to you sometime, but if you haven't received it when you get this let me know and I'll dispatch another. And when you read it let me have your frank opinion of each piece. You have read "Ballad of Bride and Groom" and I have already incorporated your suggestions there. I think there is a spot or so yet that needs trimming up somehow, and I'll get around to it before reprinting in a full collection some of these years. Perhaps it is merely stubbornness in me but I persist it being about as fond of it as anything I have done. I don't believe you have seen one or two of the others, "The Farewell," which you will trace to Steve, of course, and the final version of *Moab* itself. You have seen "Oglethorpe," "Lost Shoes," and "I'll Do As Much For My True Love."

No, there has been no postponement of the publication date of *Herbs.* It comes off in January, the exact day not specified. I should be receiving advance copies any day now. Dutton has announced it in their catalog with preposterous claims of perfection and all that sort of thing, "Reading this novel is a magnificent experience" etc. which sort of irks me. But if they have faith in it maybe they'll plug it on the market. I have had the reaction of Frank Daniel, and Russell Lord and several others to the novel. It has all been exceedingly gratifying. I hope it is not cried-up too much, because damned if I know whether I can better it next time or not. I doubt it. It is a pretty good thing, and it cost me no end of energy; In fact, so much I don't think there is anything else in my head I am willing to give as much as I did *Herbs.* I have already signed a contract for a second novel, have spent the first installment of advance royalty, and have about a twentieth of it written. This one is a good idea but I am weary at the moment. The title is *Tents Toward Sodom,* and the epigraph comes from Genesis as you would know: Abram, he hadn't become Abraham yet, dwelled in Canaan, and Lot dwelled in the cities of the plain and pitched his tent toward Sodom. The theme is the compulsion toward evil, which I take it is in all men, and the particular culminating evil in this case it suggested by the last word in the title, which, incidentally, is the symbol of evil and only by the way the symbol of perversion. There is the making of a tremendously dramatic story in that idea and theme, and I guess I'll get an honest creature. I've got to be in Atlanta on the 11th, and again twice in January, once for a luncheon for me by the Georgia Education Exchange, which is a group of old hens and disgruntled university people who have nothing better to do than meet here and there and make endless speeches about education. I am a sectional vice-p. by courtesy. Again for a party the manuscript club is pitching. I wouldn't join, I'm a non-joiner, and like Markham's circle they outwitted me. They made me an honorary member. I assume I may be asked to autograph at some of the book stores but there are no invitations and no plans yet.

But more yet. I am joining your profession briefly this summer. I am going to conduct a course in verse writing and one in the short story at the University of California summer session from June 19th through August 11. That is, at Lost Angels. I'm damned if I know why I accepted except that I always felt I'd end up in California doing some nonsensical thing. I can manage the verse writing well enough, but the short story is a different matter. I never wrote but one in my life, and it is being published in the *Chicago Review.* I think I mentioned it to you once. It is a "Logical Jew." The idea is good but I am by no means proud of the execution. I'll send you a copy for criticism when it comes out. The compensation at UOCA is 450 per four weeks plus three hundred bucks traveling expenses. Perhaps it was the traveling expenses that did it. I always wanted to make a jaunt across the continent. The trouble is that once I get there, there is no telling when I'll get away. John Vincent of the Music Department is the guy who is behind all this. He wants to get me there to work on an opera with him. He has just set a Christmas poem of mine, which he expects to go over well a year from this Christmas. It is too late now to get a choral arrangement printed for the trade.

I believe I am run down, and the night advancing toward morning.

Faithfully,

Reece

My regards to Miss Jane. I think she knows he is one of the names in "My Lombi Baut of Life."

B.

[1950 ?]

Dear G. B.:

I have always been so pleased to hear from you that I never could pay you back in your own coin of laggard writing, but it looks like this time I have done very well by myself in that respect. Actually the circumstances under which I have bungled through the last two or three months have been not very conducive to writing of any sort. I have been so busy, and when not busy there has been so much illness here that it keeps me all torn up, and I can't make heads or tails of things after getting away from a set routine for awhile.

My mother has been very ill for the last three weeks. She has had several hemorrhages, and while they are not necessarily dangerous, they are the most upsetting things I can imagine. She is better right now, else I would still be in the stew that has seethed around in me for the last three or four weeks.

As I may or may not have told you, I had been at work on the novel I signed a contract to deliver to Dutton by Sept. 1st, before I got upset by the illness of my mother. I had completed about half of it in semi-final form, but now I am stuck. I hate work of any sort that has to be sustained for any length of time. I guess I was born lazy. At least I have developed into a very lazy person mentally. I will do anything under heaven to keep from getting to work. I have read dozens of books when I should have been working on my own. I have even written a few poems lately to avoid working in prose. I haven't the faintest notion whether or not I'll meet my deadline, but if not, Dutton will just have to postpone publication date, unless they want to publish an unwritten novel which would be a noteworthy feat in itself.

Your last letter was a little cynical, though I should be the last person in the world to take note of the fact. Actually, you nor I (neither of us, that is,) is a cynical person basically. We have merely been betrayed by our ideals; and as far as that is concerned that may be a pretty good definition of a cynic. I think perhaps I was first attracted to you by your basic decency and I have no reason to believe that has altered. I wish though that I could see more of you. Do you and June plan to come up about commencement time at YHC? I feel a complete stranger over there now, but I hope you have enough interest left in that place to bring you up. As for that matter you could come up without any reason and it wouldn't offend me at all.

I think I have a fit of spring fever on now. It rained here yesterday and the day before, and today is extraordinarily beautiful, warm and sunshiny, and I am engulfed in a feeling of lassitude. It is pleasant if you can give yourself over to it, but I am so far behind with my correspondence and other commitments I feel guilty if I don't spend every available moment working. Perhaps sometime, though I haven't much hopes of it, I'll have enough money to indulge my lazy streak for a while. If I ever reach to that blissful state I think I could wish life would last forever. However, I'd have to follow the sun, because in the cold of winter my best impulses freeze out and it takes warm weather to thaw them out again. I think if the preachers preached hell as a cold place I'd be more eager to avoid it.

How is school, and how are you and June? You might let me hear from you before too long without getting writer's cramp. Personally the best cure I ever found for that was to keep on writing.

Faithfully,

Reece

Dear G. B.:

This will probably be in installments and by the time I am done it may not appear so prompt as it starts off. That is to say I got you letter today, hence this if finished now would appear indecently prompt. I am indebted to J. R. Gaskin for the idea and phrase, indecently prompt. It sort of tickled my fancy; I having always held a notion that no matter how much you might want to reply to a letter you should put it off a bit in order to appear somewhat disinterested. This, I am aware is a sort of elliptic self-defense mechanicism (I think I'll take out a copyright on that last word). Mechanism is what I mean. The only trouble with Freud is that he doesn't teach you how to spell. And speaking of Gaskin, I had a letter from him in February and he was then within about nineteen days of his discharge. So I suppose he is now out of the Navy. Greear is at home in Helen as I have probably told you before; I have told so many people so many things lately I am all confused in memory. Kenneth Crawford dropped in on me the other day. He was on his way from Florida back to Chicago where he now lives. He is also out of the navy. But I am off the subject again. Gaskin suggested that we get as many old members of the Quill club together as possible and hold a reunion. I demurred on the grounds that Little Man's death would put a damper on the proceedings. He countered with the notion that no matter how long we waited we would not be able to keep him out of our minds at such an affair, which is true enough I think. But so far there are only three of us available at the moment, Greear, Gaskin and me. That would make a pretty shabby reunion, I am afraid we would end up in tears and a lot of sentimental gibberish. We would be remembering too many absent members, some of them absent forever I suppose, though so far as I know the Q C suffered no casualty. At any rate we are letting it slide for the time being. I still think it is a good idea if we could manage to get enough of us together sometime. What do you think about it?

I am afraid this letter is going to be too long, but once I get it off my chest you won't have to put up with such ungodly epistles. Your mention of the Fort Valley lady who attended the Writer's Club breakfast (at twelve o'clock) in Macon reminds me that I met her and meant to remember her name since she was from your baliwick, but I didn't succeed. I think though her name is mentioned in some publicity the Club gathered for me and put into a scrap book (if I had been of the other sex I would have had a flower for my hat instead of the scrapbook). I met about five hundred and fifty people that day and the day before; they gave me an autograph party at the Baptist Book Store in Atlanta the day before, and all of them by name so I didn't remember a very large percentage of them. There were three or four Ft. Valleyians at the book fair in Atlanta the first of May. I retired in triumph from the book fair and have not stirred since. You ask how it feels to be acclaimed by the public. It embarrasses me something awful. Gov. Arnall praised the ballad of mine that appeared in the *Atlanta Journal* book supplement in his welcoming address at the book fair. I wanted to go through the floor when people turned around to look at where I was sitting in Dutton's box at the auditorium but like the old spiritual there was no hiding place. When Jesse Stuart spoke he said north Georgia raised neither the best corn nor the best cotton but in me had raised one of the best poets in America. The audience interrupted him by clapping loud and long. I am afraid I blushed like a new bride. I made the front page of both papers while in Atlanta for the fair, and without turning a hand. In fact I have been publicized ad nauseam in Georgia. I am enough of an egoist to get a certain amount of pleasure out of the fuss and bother, but on the other hand it irks me for total strangers to stop me on the street and say, "O, you are the new Georgia poet" as several have done in Atlanta and Gainesville. Their pleasure at having won a mental bet about whether or not I was the poet is harmless, but I resent them all the same. No one is more aware of how short is the public memory than I am and I derive a sort of cynical pleasure out of the knowledge. All feelings and situations are complicated beyond measure. That's one reason writing is so difficult, and that's why we are never certain about our feelings for another person. To make one's meaning clear would take too many qualifications. If I followed my train of thought and added every qualification that comes to mind I would end up on the judgment day qualifying my latest qualification. I am a ruthlessly faithful person on general principle, but my feelings for another person are in constant turmoil. People who know me think I lead a drab and uninteresting life; they should have to skip to my damned mental apparatus. There was an English girl studying to be a doctor who committed suicide because she could see two sides to every question. If I see only two I count myself fortunate, there are usually dozens of sides.

The notion of visiting you and June gives me pleasure, but I'll have to forego that for the time being. We are in desperate straits about a crop this year. I am still farming and will have to keep it up until I make a lot more money than I am at present. The few hundred dollars royalty I have received so far without being implemented by what we make on the farm would last about as long as Patty stayed in hell—he arrived in hell while the clock struck one and went out while the clock was still striking, that I learned from an old man who used to be a neighbor of ours-Uncle Cussin' Tom Henson. It has rained here for the last two months practically without let up. Ordinarily I would have got my turning done in the fall but last fall, I was bustling about because of *Bones* instead of staying home and tending to my knitting. I am paying for it now in mental anguish. It finally gets too late to plant corn, or anything else as for that matter, and I get almost to the point of biting my fingernails sitting on my fanny sweating it out while it rains and rains and the weeds grow waist high in the unplowed fields. If you are still in Biloxi in August, I might make it out there. In September I'll be cutting hay and so forth, and I am going to NY for a brief spell between that and corn gathering time. I met my publishers at the Atlanta book fair and the V.P.'s wife says I can live with them in their apartment and have a record player all to myself. It's funny but I find most women are impressed by the most elementary knowledge of classical music. That's the sort of knowledge mine is. I only know what I like, and as the portrait painter told the lady who said she knew what she liked, so does a cow. I find that the ladies who seek after culture with a capital C are apt to be sort of neurotic; a number of them I have bumped up against at literary teas, which I've had to endure on a few occasions, must have eunuchs for husbands. Let them get a few drinks and they fawn over you like a bitch in heat. It leaves me with a slimy feeling inside and out, I feel better about it after I've had a bath.

I am glad you like the lyrics better than the ballads. I find few people who have that much gumption. I know damn well they are better and I ought to know. If there's anything much in any of the ballads other than the title one I builded better than I knew because I wrote them because I was bored stiff with teaching school and so unhappy that I couldn't write any lyrics. I don't know why I overlooked "Winterpiece." Some I included in the original MS of *Bones* Dutton's poetry editor threw out but I didn't include that one. I haven't a copy in MS and that may be why I forgot about it. If I ever really amount to anything somebody will have a holiday going through my manuscripts and old magazines and my correspondence after I'm dead. Personally I'd hate to have the job of straightening out such a mess. By the way, I've sent the MS and work sheets, what few survive, of *Bones* to the library of the University of Buffalo by request. That library will furnish material for PhD researchers for a thousand years. They have copies of everything published by significant modern poets and manuscripts and work sheets from most of them.

I'm working on the MS of a new collection of poems. Unless I change my mind it will be called *Bow Down in Jericho* and will be about evenly divided between lyrics and ballads. I don't find enough consecutive time to do much on my novel, but I'll have to buckle down and finish it too, because I've got a good bit of publicity about it and now I'm hooked with the job whether I want to or not.

Thanks for the clipping. Did you by any chance see the *NY Herald-Tribune* review of *Bones*? The old gal who reviewed it lifted my scalp. I. L. Saloman, a Vermont poet wrote in to protest, and they've had a small controversy about it, which amuses me. I pay no attention to what reviewers say, good or bad, though the *Trib* review is the only really bad one I've received.

This, it seems to me, is enough.

Faithfully,

Reece

BLAIRSVILLE, GA.

January 26, 1950

Dear Mr. Graham:

Despite certain hitches the Atlanta parties went off well. Everything there is in hand, I believe, despite the fact that we may have got off on the wrong foot with Sarah Wheeler, whom you must know, everybody else does, but ignoring her invitation to milk me and the book on her radio program. Most of the book sellers in Atlanta dislike her; I haven't discovered why. I don't dislike anybody in particular except a number of book reviewers for the daily press who judge a book by telling how they would have written it instead of how the author did. The reviews I have seen of *Herbs* are by no means all favorable, but at least it is not being ignored. I guess I was spoiled by the reviews of *Ballad of the Bones;* except for one review they were all favorable.

What I started out to do was to request some photos for publicity purposes. Could you send me two or three in the size, say, of those sent out with the book publicity. I need one for the University of California. I was fool enough to agree to conduct two courses there during their summer session. I might also remind you gently that you promised to return the photograph I sent, when you had had copies made. I wouldn't give a damn whether or not it was returned except for the fact it isn't my property. I am getting a big kick out of the various reproductions of the picture; you'd never guess they were all from the same photo.

If anything happens in connection with *Herbs* that might mean money pass the news on to me to cheer me up. I'm broke as a hant. I need some copies of *Herbs* but I am already in debt to the sales department and hesitate to ask for further credit there. It's a nice situation when an author can't buy copies of his own book. It'd make good publicity, but of the kind I wouldn't appreciate.

When Ralph Hancock comes around give him my regards. The only celebration of the publication of my book, so far as I know, was a small one Ralph [McGill] and I managed on our own in the small hours of a morning in an Atlanta hotel.

Sincerely,

Byron Herbert Reece

BLAIRSVILLE, GA.

January 27, 1950

Dear Pratt:

At the moment I am in a sweat between the need to be utilizing the time I have free for writing and the disinclination to write. I have, as I have told you, I think, started a second novel, and now it is bad, drizzling weather here and I can do nothing else, but I can't write either. It is a hell of a feeling and wears me out. I am always torn between two loyalties, one to go on making my bread on the farm and the other to get out of my system those things I want to comment on through writing. If I could ever earn a living through writing what I want to write I'd be free and as happy as a mortal can expect to be. It is possible I may be able to do that one time, but not yet. The feeling of frustration in me is hard to bear, but I simply can't write when I'm not in the mood to do so, no matter how valuable time is. It would seem that one should be able to rest on his stroke after publishing a novel, but I am contracted and promised up to my ears and it will probably take me three years to work out from under. When that happens I'll be double and triple damned if I ever sign another contract for anything until it is finished, or commit myself to conduct any courses, the California thing is a mistake as I very well know at the time I promised to go there for the Summer, I don't know what drove me to accept except for the fact that it seems logical that one should grab all opportunities as they come, which is a false doctrine. But all this is getting us nowhere.

Thanks for the poems. I like "After The Raven" a great deal. It is moving and exciting, especially the first half of the poem. It seems to me to fall off slightly beginning with "Sometime after the raven we rode away," though I can't say exactly why I think so. The line I have just been quoting is good in itself and down to the How the old plug mule ... perhaps it is that sentence ending with the word yet that throws me. God knows I hate a lot of "poetics" but despite the implied humanity on your part revealed in those two lines they are not to my eye poetic. Don't change it merely because I take exception to those lines unless you feel yourself that my feeling for them may be just. I don't believe in letting somebody else be your judgment. Be your own judgment. I don't presume to criticize the other three poems. They are personal. I like a number of your fortunate combinations I have noticed in different poems, as "all the marvel-mechanism of the life of the other." "The Beautiful Discovery," etc. pleases me except for an unfortunate placement of one line.

With your
beauty invite
Me to the mystery and success
of your neck
and lips
... your stern
Mouth, etc.

I suggest you write it, Your stern mouth, etc. The nautical term that the word is in another sense when applied to the human anatomy makes possible an interpretation I am sure you didn't mean of even foresee. Of course when you pass on from the adjective to the noun the meaning is the same as if you wrote it as I suggest, but it is perhaps just as well not to give rise to the other interpretation at all. The poem is good and I see no reason why it shouldn't be submitted, but I am an honest creature and my honesty frequently leaves me open for blows the devious never receive. What you reveal is certainly well titled. It is the beautiful discovery that could go on all the time. The title reminds me of Patchen. There is an insight in the poem that applies to "the love that dares not speak its name," to quote Lord Douglas, too, though the position that those who know anything about that insight find themselves in amuses me no end. The natural assumption doesn't seem to be the same as that which explains how a sane man can write about an insane man with understanding. By all means save the poem. It seems I have presumed to judge the poems after all.

Herbs is being reviewed all over in the daily press. It will probably get some coverage in the magazines before long. The reviews for the most part have irked me and prodded me to defend or explain, and sometimes to insult the reviewers. A good part of the reviewers missed the boat I traveled on when I wrote the book. As far as I am concerned the book is a small perfection. There isn't a nuance in the book that came by chance. I knew what I was doing at every point and not only that but also examined and rejected other ways of doing each thing I did. Some say I have not the sense of narrative necessary to a novelist. Others say that the narrative technic is perfect. One, in the *NY Times* says the climax is realistic action of the most grotesque sort; she doesn't know my characters or she would know that the action is not only not grotesque but inevitable to the characters, another in the *Christian Century,* or *Science Monitor* I think it is, says that it is in such a minor key one can't feel the conflict. So they contradict one another and miss most of my points altogether. When I say the book is a small perfection I mean it says exactly what I meant it to say. There is room for argument of course about whether what I have said is worth saying or the way I have said it the best way. What irks me is the imputation that I did not know what I was about. I knew exactly what I was about. As I wrote in a letter you probably hadn't received when you wrote I'll send you a copy of the book as soon as I can afford some copies. Never mind returning "Crows" etc, my other copy came back to me the other day, but give me your reaction to the poem.

I've got to write a dozen or so acknowledgment letters to people who have written about the book. Let me hear from you when you have time to write.

Byron

First or Second week in April 1950

Dear Pratt:

This will be an unsatisfactory letter. I am dead tired, dog tired. I have been cutting hedges with a long blade and after you swing one of those things for nine or ten hours the sap is all gone out of you. Which reminds me of a thought I had two or three weeks ago. My brother and I have bought a tractor, and among the implements a wood saw goes with it. It was cold and we sawed wood for about four hours. If you have seen one operate you will understand how much energy it takes to keep wood to the saw (it turns about 1850 revolutions a minute). The news that night was not good, about the cold war and all that, and as I sat before the fire too tired to move I thought what a peaceful, what a virtuous world this would be if everybody had to tail a wood saw every day. And while we cannot expect everybody to do that, there is still something in the principle on which the thought operates. If people had enough work to do to keep them healthily occupied, then notions to blow up their neighbor would be considerably less likely to drive them down a blind ally to destruction. If those who think and plan and hope wars destroyed only themselves it wouldn't be so bad but I bitterly resent being involved with them, as is inevitable.

That was not what I meant to write about. I enjoyed your letter that came today, also the one that came a day or so after I mailed you my last one. I admire the two poems "Great Love" and "Possibilities." I like the latter more because it is the deeper and of wider implication. I don't know what Lape's criticism of it may have been, but it irks me for a critic to carp about points of technique, and after all, that is all that one can criticize, for the author is not to blame for the spirit of the thing. If I like the substance of a work, I leave it to the author to say it in his own way. I might as well, for really anything worth saying will be said in an individual way whether it be said through traditional or experimental techniques. What I am driving at is this: in the final analysis an author's equipment is intangible. It is himself, the sum total of his character and his emotional cast. That is if he has any integrity. If he has no integrity there is nothing to be said for him anyway.

I think your work is good. Try to keep it as tight as possible. I cannot tell you how to do it. I can only say this. In the process of creation you will <u>feel it</u> if any phrase or sentence is really out of context. Depend upon your own sensibilities. And just keep plugging away. I think it is almost, though not quite, inevitable that good work will finally come to its audience. Keep submitting to such magazines as the *Land.* I am glad to see that, or hear from you rather, that you are to have a poem in the spring number. I will also have two poems in that issue. I wish I could prevail upon you to do a novel. That is, unless you feel that the magnitude of the task would lead you to frustration. The prose of your letters often has a distinctive quality. Writing a novel does appear a frightening undertaking until it is done, and then it turns out not to have been so bad after all. I don't understand authors who write themselves out with one. I have more to say now than before I had written a novel. If I can muster the fortitude I am urging on you I intend to do a second, beginning this fall. It will probably be *Tents Toward Sodom,* and if you wish to get the lay of the land it will cover read of Lot's parting with Abraham on the uplands of Canaan. It will be a study, in fiction, of the compulsion toward evil, a theme that fascinates me in company with most other writers.

I take it from your letter that you are unhappy about love. I am not trying to pry into your affairs, it is none of my business, and besides nothing is so boring as somebody else's love affairs! I would hazard a guess though, that the miracle is not lost to you. I am not of the school who believe that you only love once. I have seen a lot of people I could have loved if I had had time and the means ... and weren't too concerned with my own ego to do so. From an intellectual point of view love is an unhealthy state of affairs. It is a sickness that wants to preserve its symptoms. I am not altogether serious, as you will judge. But, and seriously now, I have sometimes thought that love as we have come to understand the term, between sexes, as between homosexuals, is an emotional aberration. Concerning normal love, your note is much to the point. And I think homosexuality despite all the answers (which are not really answers) the novelists have given us lately, is simply a repudiation of life. It is or has been prevalent among dying societies one and all from Canaan to Greece to Rome to Germany, and since it seems to be spreading in the United States, it gives me some concern about our own culture. I do not pretend to be shocked by it. In my experience though, I have never heard of a homosexual developing in a rural area. And that, I think, is accounted for by the fact that rural people's reactions are likely to be more elemental than people's of more complex cultures. Before leaving the subject, I have read only *The Pillar and the City,* and *The Fall of Valor* of the many novels on the theme within the last few years. And they were both given to me by their publishers. I expect to read the *Christmas Tree* and *Other Voices, Other Rooms* when I get around to them.

I meant to say, and do now, that I understand your feelings as expressed in your letter. I have had them and have them myself. The pagan glory and the loss. It is all pretty involved, and I am not dead with old age myself. And if the end all things could be predicted with mathematical accuracy I would immediately blow out my brains, for life wouldn't be worth living at all at all were it robbed of its mysteries.

The passage you quote from the 91st Psalm is magnificent, of course. *The Modern Reader's Bible,* and it's like, can do wonders for the Old Testament.

But the *Revised Standard Version* plays hell with the *New*, if you will forgive the expression. It ruins its eloquence altogether, and if one hasn't sense enough to read the King James Version I think he will not get much out of the other either. I love most of Isaiah, and the book of The Preacher (All is Vanity), I cannot spell it without looking it up and that is too much trouble at the moment. The Poem beginning Remember thy creator now in the days of they youth is one of the loveliest in the language, and is one of the best extended metaphors.

I did read Rorty's poem in the March *Harper's* but for the life of me I can't remember what it was about. I think I like Thomas H. Ferrill's (sp doubtful) poem in the same issue better. I note you have a great deal of admiration for Rorty. He sometimes leaves me dangling in mid-air. At other times his insights are remarkable and aptly expressed. I am enclosing a poem of his from the last issue of the *Land* which I believe you have not seen. I once subscribed to *Harper's* but changed to *Atlantic* and regret the change. *Atlantic* rarely publishes poetry of any distinction and the stories are often mighty weak. On the Whole tomorrow is better in my view.

I'll try to send you copies of some stuff after next week. I am going to visit on the campus of the University of Georgia the 13 and 14 and will have to spend some time now getting some ideas straight in my head, since I am going to speak to three or four diverse classes besides reading at chapel.

Faithfully,

Byron

BLAIRSVILLE, GA.

May 2, 1950

Dear Pratt:

Your recent long letter was the kind I love to receive, but never earn these days. I have been meaning to write to you for a long time, but I am terribly busy now. I meant to write just after receiving your letter-before-last, when you seemed to be in a bad mood, discouraged about your writing and low generally. I think you have come out of it, from the tone of your last letter. At least about your writing. Of course your writing is over the edge, whatever edge might mean. That is to say that any writing that's worth a damn is out of the ordinary, and I know of no place from which extraordinary writing shall proceed except from an extraordinary personality. I don't know or know of your creative writing teacher, and I should not like to say anything that would damage the possibility of your learning from her, it is a "her" isn't it? But I wish she would consider the fact that the method of telling also "shows" a great deal. I believe in showing too, since I believe in "dramatic" literature, but I also believe in allowing an original bent to go undamaged. Anyway, all writers have to thresh out their own problems, for though technique can be taught and learned, there is a great gap between the bare essentials of technique and accomplishment. Practice makes perfect, and that is about the extent of what we can do to learn to write. I am happy that my assignment a UCLA is for only two months. I can scarcely do a great deal of damage to talent, in case any appears in my course there, in two months.

I had the pleasure of hearing Toscanini and the NBC Symphony perform in concert at the Municipal Auditorium in Atlanta on the 22nd of April. Brahm's first and Schubert's unfinished were the principal works, and though both of them are high up on my list of preferred music, I recall scarcely anything of the music. I was too busy concentrating on Toscanini himself. He is the only "sole thing of its kind" I ever witnessed in action. There were once two great men I wanted to see in the flesh. I have now seen one of them. The other is Albert Schweitzer. I think I much prefer my music canned ordinarily. I was brought up on the record and not in the concert hall. With a good reproduction system, there is not too much missing from the recorded music, and the orchestra and conductor do not come between you and the music when the record is playing.

Herbs continues to get good reviews and sells very indifferently. I'll make little beyond the advance unless something unforeseen turns up, like a sale to the movies. I would cheerfully sell *Herbs* to the movies and never give a thought to what they might make of it. I learned long ago that books and movie based on books are two different matters. I need money to allow me to go on with my work. Dutton is publishing my second full collection of poems *Bow Down In Jericho* on the 17 of July. That will give me two publications in the year 1950. It may be ten years before I offer a third collection of poetry. I am to finish a second novel by the first of next January. *Jericho* contains some of my very best work in the field of poetry, especially the ballad, and perhaps the sonnet. My lyrics, while some of them are rather individual and all competent, are nothing to crow about. A few of them may live for awhile. At best a poet will be remembered, by three or four poems. We could put the whole of our lyric heritage in one rather small book and never miss what was left out. Dutton's poetry editor said of *Jericho*, "The book is magnificent. The Biblical ballads, especially the David and Jonathan sequence, are marvelously wrought and should live forever." My first reaction on reading that was: Forever is a long time.

When I get to Los Angeles I'll pick up a copy of *Herbs* and send you. I wish I could do it now, but I simply haven't the money to spare. It amuses me, in a bitter sort of way, that I most borrow the money to take me to California. I'll see that you get a copy of *Jericho* straight off. I'll be on a fairly decent salary when it appears.

This is too brief, but I've got to get some sleep. Let me hear from you as often as you find time to write. I wish I was having you as a student at UCLA. The cost of a summer session, including board is about $256.00. How about it?

Faithfully,

Byron

2/19/51

Dear Pratt:

Dutton made a thousand of these, and I've been holding this until I heard from you. I am doing nothing of interest or importance at the moment. I am suffering from reluctance to get on with the novel. I've done a good bit of poetry this winter, some good some not. I've been trying to sell it with no spectacular results. I have sold three or four to the *Land,* four to *Ga. Review,* one or so to *Recurrence*, a paying little mag. published in Los Angeles. I have three new ballads, but I'm unable to palm them off on anybody that pays. I'll see Edward Weeks of *Atlantic* next week at Athens, might bull doze him into taking one. I'm going to Cleveland, Ohio, either in March or April to read and speak to Ohio Poetry Society. I'm supposed to finish the novel by April 1st, but won't make it again. Dutton's hope I'll win a Pulitzer Prize or National Dove Award for Poetry, and am trying to impress the judges. I hope so too, but expect no such good fortune. I have been mixing cement today—and it strikes me it will probably endure longer than I or any literary work. Be that as it may, I am tired and feeling very dull. Let me hear from you as often as you can find time and energy to write. Your present schedule seems pretty full to me.

Faithfully,

Byron

BLAIRSVILLE, GA.

February 4, 1952

Dear Gaskin:

I don't know how my intention to write you as soon as I received your letter in December got shunted into now, but so it did. There isn't much to report from this angle of the compass right now. I have a new collection of poetry in the hands of Dutton and they will publish it in late summer or early fall under the title *A Song of Joy and Other Poems*. That cleared my clutter of poetry, and now I am off on a sort of new tack, in poetry, but it yet remains to be seen if anything of importance will come of it. As for that second novel it got snagged or aground about this time last year and I have not done a thing on it since. It is something like half done, what of it is written pleases me well enough, though to tell the truth I am reluctant to finish it. I have applied for a Guggenheim Fellowship and I am now waiting on news of the outcome of that before I get back to work on the novel. I think perhaps I'll get one. I gave, among others, four former Fellows as references. But you never can tell. The announcement of fellows for 1952 will be made late in March.

My family, my parents I should say, are in ill health and I have all the farm work and all the chores on my hands. All in all it is a pretty hard physical drag and I don't have much energy left for writing, hence my application for the Guggenheim. I continue to earn practically nothing from my books. *Herbs* is now out of print, though I have a number of copies on hand here. *Jericho* hasn't sold like *Bones* did, though it got a uniformly good press. This, they tell me, is a bad time for selling books. I hope that is the reason that the sales of *J* are not up to snuff, comparatively speaking. *Song of Joy*, I think, will stand a pretty good chance at "The trial by market everything must come to," to quote or paraphrase Frost.

I can well imagine your teaching forces you to do a lot of work, but I doubt if you are in it over your head. It is good to hear that the work for the degree is all over. Do you have any plans for publication of the thesis? It seems to me there should be room for it somewhere.

Give my regards to Miss Jane. I'd like to see the young one. When you are up this way sometime maybe you could bring her by for a visit. I hear nothing from most of our YHC friends, though I had a letter from the former Ruth Bently, I've forgotten her married name, from Columbus, Ohio. Greear is in Japan in the Air Force and his wife is on the point of dragging their three children all those miserable miles to join him. Broadrick is also in the A.F. Jack

I. Biles visits me once or twice each summer. He is working on his masters at Emory. I saw Raymond Cook last Sunday. He is teaching English at Emory. I spoke to the preachers there last summer. You can always depend on me to wind up the preachers.

Faithfully,

Reece

BLAIRSVILLE, GA.

March 9, 1952

Mr. Elliott Graham, Publicity Director

E. P. Dutton & Co., Inc.

300 Fourth Avenue, New York 10, N.Y.

Dear Elliott:

It must be provoking at times to be a publicity director, especially when it comes to preparing catalog and jacket material about people to whom nothing exciting ever happens. I don't believe I have any information to speak of that you don't have already. Of the things that have happened to me since the publication of *Bow Down in Jericho* these might be mentioned: In the summer of 1950 I conducted courses in the short story and verse writing at the University of California at Los Angeles. Last June I was awarded the Georgia Writers Association's Achievement award in fiction for *Better a Dinner of Herbs* and their Award in poetry with *Bow Down in Jericho.* At the same time I received the Trosdal-Barrow Award for poetry with *Bow Down in Jericho*. I am frequently hooked on judging committees and for readings from my verse, especially in the South.

You have copies of the reviews of my previously published books, and I'm sure you are better at selecting the right things from them than I am. I am at work on a second novel and have at least one other planned, besides two or three poetry projects that occupy me off and on. I still work the farm on Wolf Creek, and I often find myself over-extended and feeling very much akin to the insect known to all children as a "granddaddy" who must have trouble figuring out which way he is going since his legs point in all directions at once.

I have applied for a Guggenheim Fellowship to aid me in bringing my second novel to completion. You can never tell about those things until the scores are posted. I hope I will be awarded one; I'll know about that by the last of March and will catch you up on that as soon as I hear.

Personally I am sick of the jacket photo on *Better a Dinner of Herbs*. If you need a photograph and are willing to process a new one (it will have to be copied because it isn't gloss) say the word and I'll send one that suits me better than the old one. This is not a terribly important matter, I know, and I won't press it.

If there is anything else I can do to cooperate, let me know.

Sincerely,

Byron Herbert Reece

P.S. I need a photograph, anything you have available, for my old college to print among "interesting graduates" in this year's annual.

B.

P.P.S. My first short story was published today in the *Atlanta Journal & Constitution Magazine.*

BLAIRSVILLE, GA.

September 6, 1952

Mr. Elliott Graham, Publicity Director

E.P. Dutton & Co.

New York, N.Y.

Dear Elliott:

Since it is notorious that most book reviewers don't have sense enough to think for themselves, especially those who review for that contemptible contemptuous last refuge of the critical cliché, the *Saturday Review,* the quote from *Newsweek* on the jacket of *Joy* has probably done the book a huge disservice, and should there ever be an occasion to reprint it, I think it should be dropped. I am sick and tired of the theme song of candid derivation the other reviewers have picked up from Robert Cantwell. God knows I have never read Whittier, I have a good natured contempt for Longfellow, I am a dozen cuts below Blake and a lot of people have either read Frost wrong or me wrong or neither of us at all.

Enclosed is a copy of a letter I have written to the editor of the *Saturday Review.* It may be bad policy to object to their review but I don't give a damn if it is. Nobody, so far as I know, is grateful for their condescending glance in the direction of poetry every three of four months anyway. And the person who is capable of writing such blather as the headnote to the poetry reviews in the Sept. 6 issue ought to railroaded out of the English language. I'd like to know what in the name of God the poets and their critics were doing in the mountains and at the seashore if not gathering clams or cutting acid wood to earn their livings; I have never in my time heard of a person of either breed who has grown opulent enough from the practice of his art to take a vacation. As for me I am used to earning my bread by the sweat of my brow, a phrase derived from Genesis, and I can do it just as well without the approval of the *Saturday Review.* Some of these days I am going to write an ode to the long nose of the North down which all Southern writers are stared condescendingly at, meanwhile I am.

Yours Sincerely,

Byron Herbert Reece

Sunday, March 8, 1953

Dear Pratt:

Think of the good I could have done for myself by visiting you there, but many things have prevented it. My work is not going very well, for one thing, and I am trying to stretch the Guggenheim as far as possible, which I can do best by staying here where my expenses are at least not as great as they would be elsewhere. My parents continue ill, have had the flu and been awfully close to death two or three times. It is hard to live with people after they get old and ill and watch them wearing away.

I do intermittent work on the novel and continue to write poetry when the spirit moves, and sometimes when it doesn't. I just sold the *Sat Eve Post* a short lyric, which is nothing to shout about but better than a lot of the stuff they publish. I don't sell many poems. I don't even try. The income tax is so great on even small earnings if one is single it is highly discouraging. Do you have trouble in that direction too?

It is good to know of Powell's interest in my work. If I had received your letter a day or two earlier I could have contributed several issues of *Trails* but unfortunately I had given them away, along with any number of issues of various and sundry small magazines. I also gave away a whole batch of *Lands,* but since I am a member I do get it regularly, and will remember to send you the next issue when I am through with it. I would like to keep a lot of things like magazines and so on, but after fifteen or twenty years they accumulate until you have such a storage problem you just chunk them out in the handiest direction without even examining. As I grow older I lighten the cumberances, so that if I live to be very old, outside of my library, which I will leave to some college, I will approach eternity traveling light. Incidentally, *Bones* and *Better a Dinner of Herbs* are out of print and if Mr. Powell can't find copies tell him to get in touch with me. I have several copies of each. And did you ever get a copy of *Song of Joy*? If not let me know and I'll send one.

I'm no authority on the matter but I think an outright purchase contract is for all rights. In other words, you wouldn't realize anything on a second edition or on sale of serial or reprint rights. Of course no contract has to be in any set form. You could, if the other party were willing, sell rights to a first edition outright and include in the contract clauses to reserve to you a certain percentage of any subsequent earnings such as royalty on second edition and sale of serial or reprint rights. You had better contact Swallow or somebody before you enter such a contract. I think it is generally better to publish on a regular royalty basis if possible. If not, if you finance publication yourself you retain all rights. Of course outright purchase is predicated on the notion that the risk involved in realizing a profit off a book about balances out with the chance of making a killing on regular trade copies plus sale of other rights in the material.

You speak of Powell's association with *Arizona Quarterly* in past tense. Is he no longer editor, or is the magazine no longer published. I never saw but three or four issues. One Raymund sent me, a couple I bought somewhere and one E.V. Griffith sent me with a friend's work in it.

I got a devil of a bad review of *Joy* in the latest issue of *Voices.* Others that I have seen have been mostly good. At least it gets mention in all of the summations of the year's poetry. The daily press is always favorable, the middlebrows mostly so. The highbrows usually ignore me. It is selling slowly, about three hundred copies from July to October, the period over which I have had a royalty report. Of course no one expects poetry to sell these days. *Bones* sold around five thousand copies before it went out of print, and it is somewhat discouraging to have subsequent volumes sell less than a first.

I have the offer of a residence Fellowship at Huntington Hartford in LA. if I should take it I would either go or come by Tucson. I rather doubt that I will take it, but might possibly. I've got to make up my mind soon. Is your mother still with you there? Let me hear from you.

Faithfully,

Byron

Toward the last of February 1954

Dear Pratt:

I was beginning to wonder what had happened to you, though I suspected you might be away from home. I was glad to have your letter, and I'd like to have your report on your visit with Robinson Jeffers. He and I might quarrel splendidly, but I don't think we'd find much on which to agree.

I have read few of the books you asked about, so can't tell you anything about them specifically. If I remember correctly, most or all of them with the exception of Rukeyser, are not D. titles. I have never read anything by Albert; but I'll bet you the price of a copy of his book that it is free verse. Howard Baker usually writes in strict form. He is much admired in some quarters. John Berryman is pretty readable. He uses form and free forms, which reads queerly I know, but you get what I mean. Malcolm Cowly can be damn good when he feels like it, and likewise pretty lax and meaningless. He is one who had great promise and failed to develop, in the consensus of critical opinion which means little, + Richard Eberhart is very difficult, writes in free forms, and stinks, for my money. Flannery has had a change of heart. She started out as a lukewarm traditionalist and later opaqued up her work. She published two volumes, both of which I've read and forgotten. Muriel Rukeyser was a revolutionary in the thirties and was obsessed with images of flight-literal, in planes and quarries, and daughters torn between the love for their rich fathers and their poor, poor fellows. She has a new book out but it isn't raising the hue and cry her first two or three did-which may mean it is better. I don't trust people who preach socialism and own Packards. That was about the size of what all the infants terrible of the Rev. 30's did. They had to have something to write about. Rukeyser, though, has written some excellent poems of one breed and another undoubtedly. I suppose I have read a-half dozen poems by Ivor Winters, altogether. He writes in both set and free forms, preferring the former. Winters is certainly the closest thing we have to a great critic, though he has not yet suspected the fact that he isn't God. I have never been able to work up any enthusiasm for the few poems of Theodore Rilke I've read. He has a very fine reputation, though I think his influence has been mostly bad, his young disciples, pursuing his demonic strain beyond where it leaves the borders of comprehensiveness. Kenneth Patchen had exciting surface (which can be said for most moderns), but it's mostly sound and fury signifying nothing. "Teeth of the Lion," "Cloth of the Tempest," etc. He has written some disturbing prose, but lately published a lousy little novel of love tailored to the specifications of *Woman's Home Companion,* where it appeared. Robert Penn Warren is a sort of undecided classicist, and a better prose writer than poet. Did I ever mention

Johann Christian Friedrich Holderlin? He was a schoolmaster for a while but went mad early in life. I own a copy of his poems translated by Prockosh (however you spell him), but the translations aren't very lively. Incidentally, I have a copy of translations of four poems of Rimbaud by Ben Belitt, and wonder what all the to-do over Rimbaud was about in the first place. A writer has his intuition or he has nothing at all, but a purely demonic poet is about as useful as any other mad man.

All the freely spent opinions above may leave you thinking I haven't much regard for modern poetry. The truth of the matter is I have not. Prose is a much more satisfying field. You dump up against so few stylists in a lifetime of prose reading, so your expectations are not so hard to meet with there. Yet I live to write my own sort of poetry and hate writing prose, which I probably do better.

You once mentioned re-reading my letters, which is a compliment, but I meant to warn you that over an extended period you may find me full of contradictions. At the moment, from example, I am absolutely exhausted from extended loss of sleep. Sitting up nights with my mother who has been dangerously ill this week, hemorrhaging at the lungs, and I am not in the mood to be impressed by anything. If I felt well I could find something to praise in each of the poets mentioned.

I am surprised that Lape keeps wanting you to change poems. Some of the poems that appear in *Trails* are abominable, technically, and while this is not in least to suggest that yours are so, I don't see why he would balk at a minor structural fact when he has shut his eyes to so many of them. Nobody had a right to the say-so of the content of a poem but yourself.

Lately I have acquired 2 new albums of records. One is the S. No. 5 by Beethoven, the NBC Toscanini version. The interpretation is marvelous, but the record surfaces and the reproduction in general rotten. I was horribly disappointed to find that Victor had done such a poor job of pressing. I suspected at first that mine was merely a bad copy but Kolokin in *Sat.-Rev.* "Saturday Review of Recordings" says that they are all bad, though he affirms that the interpretation is not likely even to be equaled. The other album is Rachmaninoff's concerto No. 2 in E minor. It is altogether wonderful, the playing by Rubenstein and technically, I have been looking for a recording of Haydn's 102 B flat Symphony but have not been able to locate it.

I'll have to stop here. It's toward three in the morning and my eyes ache and my mind is only half at home.

Faithfully,

Byron

BYRON HERBERT REECE
ROUTE ONE
BLAIRSVILLE, GEORGIA

July 29, 1954

Dear Pratt:

Thanks for your letters. I hardly know where to begin to answer them. (I used to have a rage for order, to appropriate somebody's title.) Anyway, I am back home though by no means well. I stayed in the sanatorium (however you may choose to spell it, a spade is a spade) for five months and got a treatment of drugs started, which I continue here at home. My latest x-ray shows that all cavitations in my lung have closed and unless I break down again I should be all right eventually. My trouble was confined to the top of my left lung, and there were several small pits, no large cavity. I took strep and PAS for six months. Now I've been taken off strep and put on INAH because I was becoming over-sensitive to strep. It always threw me for a loop anyway. The trouble is I still have no energy. I think it is due as much to low blood pressure and nervous exhaustion as much as it is to TB. (For a while I was awfully sensitive about that short for tuberculosis.)

I've managed to get a little work done, not much. I've finished a ms of poetry which Dutton will publish in the spring as *The Season of Flesh*. I've turned in a quarter of the manuscript of my novel and have almost a second quarter typed. The whole thing is written in rough draft, but I always revise in making a final copy, so can't turn it over to a typist and save myself a lot of hard work. The poetry won't make me any money, maybe seventy-five dollars a year or something like that. I've done pretty well with the novel even before it is published considering the fact that I had a Guggenheim on it. I doubt if it sells enough copies after publication to earn the advance royalty.

Yes, I know the lounge lizards in charge of the poetry in the University quarterlies. I am contemptuous of them, which stymies them completely because it is in attitude they have reserved for me and all of my ilk. I'll win in the long run and they know it. It is they who have murdered poetry and the sale of it, and I don't give a damn how much they look down their long noses at my work, it frames recognizable human experience, and those poems of mine which are well made will endure. Of course as Auden has remarked any poet has only a handful of poems for which he can be grateful no matter how extensive his production. I know what you mean when you say the editors think a book should be uniform, but it should be no such thing in the sense that all the poems are of the same attitude. The poem should govern the attitude, not the attitude the poem. you should have your religious and sensual poems all in the same collection. As a matter of fact, there isn't much difference between the two since religion was invented as a substitute for love, and love is always sensual inasmuch as we are sentient beings. I am interested in what Unamuno says about compassion, though I think maybe he has his order reversed. I have approached a person in the opposite direction at least, first compassion, then spiritual love and then physical love. I hated life at the sanatorium because it was a violation of human dignity, and because I had compassion for my fellow victims I had a great deal of respect for personality.

I read Haniel Long's *Walt Whitman and the Springs of Courage* many years ago. And incidentally I think the scholarship of the average academic today is mostly an escape from life. It is of course necessary to be an authority on something in order to hold a job at a college. The only integrated intellectual I've met in the last few years was Blake Nevius of UCLA. A year or so ago he published the first full length study of the work of Edith Wharton. He's been in Europe as a lecturer in American Literature at one of the formerly great German universities, I've forgotten which at the moment. He was a nice, personable young guy who didn't seem to find it necessary to impress anybody with his knowledge.

Thank Des Powell for this generosity for me. I might possibly get out to Tucson this winter, but it doesn't look like a sure thing now. I'm financially in a bad fix and as soon as I'm able I'll have to get a job and get some debts paid. I have a pretty good standing offer from Emory University. And I can always go back to teaching English at Young Harris College. I think I've told you I was teaching there when I first broke down. I made the same mistake there as I always do in my teaching forays, let a student get too close to me, or vice versa, I've never figured which. Anyway this time it was a boy and the worst that can come of it is to lose him to separation. He goes into the army this month. After two years there he will be in school an additional four. By the time he is ready to enter life on his own we will have grown away from each other, which is probably just as well. But I haven't much strength to spare for losing people who are dear to me.

Anyway, let me hear from you when you have the time and inclination. Of course if it should work out I can get out there I'll contact you.

Faithfully,

Byron

December 3, 1954

Dear Mildred:

I'll ask Dutton to send you a review copy of the book right away. I think Ray Shockley of the *Journal* assigns books for review for the Atlanta papers, but mention anywhere besides on the book page would be good if you wanted to hold Leo to his word. I'll be more than happy for you to review it wherever. I couldn't wish myself in better hands.

It was good to see all of you, too. Otherwise I wouldn't have waited. (I did of course enjoy visiting with Josh and Kathy and Mr. Greear, also their small one.)

We would be glad to have you come anytime you could for lunch and the day. Do you want it to be specific? If so, let me hear.

I read *Kappa* with a deal of enjoyment. I also took the liberty of mending the dust jacket. Torn things bother me. I always get involved in trying to patch up souls, too, though I should have better sense. I usually end up by rending my own.

I've thought and thought and thought about it, and for the life of me I just can't be a Fundamentalist. Would you say the fact that all religions began the same way, in primitive belief in magic, through ancestor worship, to a concept of a primary god, does nothing to damage your case? I don't want to influence anyone's religious belief. As I told my students, if there is comfort in your belief, hold on to it, there's none in mine. But I'd rather be comfortless than defrauded. I really have a terrible regard for the truth.

Love to you all.

Byron

BYRON HERBERT REECE
ROUTE ONE
BLAIRSVILLE, GEORGIA

February 11, 1955

Dear Mildred:

Several weeks ago Dutton's promotion dept. said they would be glad to send you a review copy of *Season of Flesh*. If they did and if you make mention of it I'll appreciate a copy of said mention.

How are you all? I guess I am all right, but nervous and bored blind. I finished the novel on the last day of the old year but one, since I have had nothing to do. Worse, I can't seem to scare up anything to do that I can do which at the same time would be profitable. So I guess I'll sign a contract for another book. I can still write even if it doesn't profit me much. Incidentally, the powers that be at Dutton asked to change the title in order to make the book easier to promote. So I gave them an alternative, *The Hawk and the Sun*, which is what it will be known by. They say they have hopes of promoting it successfully, and I hope they are right.

Has Philip seen the January copy of *Atlantic Monthly*? It has quite a supplementary section on Japan, which I found very interesting. If he hasn't seen it let me know and I'll send my copy along.

Or better still, he might drop by and pick it up, and bring the family.

Love to you all.

Sincerely,

Byron

BYRON HERBERT REECE
ROUTE ONE
BLAIRSVILLE, GEORGIA

April 20, 1955

Dear Mildred:

Thank you for your letter and your note. I am returning herewith your "terrific." Maybe you don't save such things. Me, I seldom get a "terrific."

I have a cold in my chest, which is painful and damaging, and I am dull.

Philip deserves a credit line if he made something of a photo of the present subject. I always did maintain, though, that one who had sense enough not to pose the subject stood a pretty good chance of getting a decent picture. I like "truthful" pictures whether or not they flatter me. It is hard to get flattered at my age anyway.

This is Tuesday night. I have not received a copy of the *Times* yet. Maybe they will send the whole series together. It has been my experience that newspapers are constitutionally opposed to sending clippings (or papers) to subjects, so if they don't come through in a reasonable length of time could you rustle me up a copy or so? I'll look forward to your last article in the series particularly.

I hope you make the *CSM.*

I'll be glad to follow George Porter's wishes about the photo. As for that, I'd like to get a new one from Dutton for the novel jacket if they haven't already printed it. In case they did use one of course we would insist on a credit line for P.

Beethoven <u>is</u> the greatest composer. But I like a lot of Mozart. (He had a most logical and orderly mind, though a little complicated.) I also like a lot of Haydn, a little of Brahms, all I ever heard of Bach. (There is a chapter in the forthcoming novel which begins: In the Brophy's parlor a pupil practiced an air of Bach's, a little two part invention that stated a theme of pure joy and then repeated itself like a marvelous bird enchanted by its own song.) I like a few of those unspellable Russians, especially Tschiakowsky's 6th, which I understand, and which most people don't. (The wages of syntax is beyond my grammatical purse.) I like one or two of the early French, Rameau (approximately) for one.

Well, I've run out of energy. Best to you all.

Byron

June 11, or thereabouts

Dear Mildred:

I'm the least busy person I know these days, and I'm always in the mood for good company, which is to say you. I'll be happy to see you any day, afternoon or forenoon, which is convenient for you next week. On any day save Saturday, when a person by the name of Louise Duggar who is assistant ed of *Progressive Farmer* is coming to interview me. That wouldn't be any fun for you. (Me neither. I like to talk to people I know.)

My state is comatose. Nothing moves me but a faint hope of going to work in the Fall. I have the job if I can manage to get well enough to fill it. It's the Emory thing. There wouldn't be so very much work to it, but I operate at high tension when at all and no matter how ineffectually. We'll see.

Give my regards to your creepers and crawlers and of whatever motive mode.

Faithfully,

Byron

Friday Night

Dear Mildred:

First, let me thank thee and thy house for a very pleasant visit. I meant to do so earlier, but the little work I must do and my lethargy keeps me always behind schedule. That plus a rather constant sense that in the long view things matter very little either yea or nay. I am aware that we live in the short view, but am not very successful at it. I did enjoy being with you all. So thanks.

I wrote in the date of the publication of my first poem (which I missed by a year, I think, but it doesn't matter) and perhaps made one other very minor correction, which I disremember, in the first copy and sent it on to the *Daily Times.* (That is, I will Saturday Morning. It is already sealed.)

(This is Saturday morning, and I will get the envelope off to the *Times* and this one back to you. You can see my scribbling in the enclosed copy, so there is no need to comment on that.)

I am not averse to the idea of an autographing in absentia, nor to a tape-recorded interview. Whatever would please you and the parties concerned. I don't mean that like it might sound. I know that you suggested them for <u>my</u> benefit, and I appreciate your thoughtfulness.

Will you send me a couple of copies of each installment of the *Times* piece if it isn't too much trouble? I want to keep one, and I want to rub it in on Dutton's promotion director when I write for a copy of *Flesh* for you, by sending them (he, she or it) a copy. Incidentally, and I think this is more than incidental; you have been very accurate in your transcription of me. I really don't mind if you say straight out that I am at present an agnostic. But I don't think it is quite safe among the average citizens, I don't mind being unsafe, though. I sometimes enjoy the role of heretic.

I'll be delighted to be plagued by mail from you. Give Philip and the children my love, and keep your portion for yourself.

Faithfully,

Byron

BYRON HERBERT REECE
ROUTE ONE
BLAIRSVILLE, GEORGIA

June 17, 1955

Dear Pratt:

It is good that you reminded me when I wrote last (last July) for I had forgotten, and so would have had no idea where to begin to catch you up on my activities, if one can call them that. My life has been mostly a confusion of waste, especially during the past six months. My mother died last August 30, 1954. Death being so irrevocable I can accept it, though the loss of a loved one is no less for the fact that it is beyond helping. As for my own health, I'm still here at home following a pretty rigid regimen of pills and rest. I never really rest but at least I keep my body still for hours at a time. I had a terrific check-up at Emory University hospital a couple of months or more ago, and the verdict is that I'm doing fine as far as healing of the lesions in my lung is concerned. They predicted at the time that another couple of months should see me whole. I am due now for another check-up and will get it soon. Emory also said there wasn't a thing in the world wrong with me, organically, except TB. (That's enough.) I don't feel at all well, but I suppose it will take me a good long while to work back into a feeling of strength. When I stay up two or three hours I feel as if I might collapse, and my back aches to beat the devil. Anyway, enough about my ills.

You have probably read *SR's* review of *Season of Flesh* by now. Beaudoin's review first appeared in the *Memphis Commercial Appeal* and I dislike *SR* posing as a fresh review medium while reprinting reviews. I also felt the inference or implication that I'm dishonest unfair and I wrote the editor protesting the implication. Nothing will come of it. I wrote the bastards once before but they wouldn't print my letter. I never protested a review in my life except one in *Voices* except those that appear in the *Saturday Review.* I think I get my feathers up because they are so smug. I think *SR* is a very mediocre journal. I could write most of their reviews with my left hand with my eyes shut. So what have they got to be so uppity about? Generally *Season* has had a very good critical reception. Edward M. Case, whose reviews are syndicated, and so get wider distribution than *SR's* says I am the greatest contemporary poet with the possible exception of Frost. He names a fairly extensive list of the poems as being unsurpassed by any contemporary poetry. You realize of course that I am as much as possible detached. I don't take either Mr. Case or the *Saturday Review* seriously. Or better, their opinions don't engage me except *SR's* on the point of personal honesty. My business is to write as well as I can without reference to the opinion of critics or reviewers. Of course I am gratified by a good opinion of my work and I'm angered at deliberate misinterpretation of my work. I'm always getting my skull cracked between the two current schools of thought about poetry. The traditionalists take the opportunity to berate the modernists while praising me. The modernists try to break my skull in order to discredit the traditionalists. When I am rationally doing my work I say to hell with both camps, a plague on both your houses, and go on about my business. The *SR* review was in the May 21 issue in case you have not seen it and want to look it up.

Beyond the book of verse, I have a novel coming out the 4th of August. It is called *The Hawk and the Sun*. I junked the title under which it was written, *Tents Toward Sodom,* at the suggestion of Dutton. It is a matter of personal gratification I guess to insist that the new title was mine, too. Anyway, the novel is racial in theme and will probably get a hell of a bad press in the South. I don't give a damn if it does. It is a good novel within its limits. And you can't put everything into one book. I got *Season* and *Hawk* both together in 1954, while I was recuperating. I completely rewrote the novel from the beginning chapters I wrote several years ago. I finished the novel on the last day of the year. Since that time I have written nothing at all, which accounts no doubt for the feeling of confused waste that has overtaken me. I have a contract for a new novel but don't feel able to get into it yet. I don't mean physically, though that's part of it; I don't feel the story enough yet to start writing it. I've got to mull it over awhile.

It is good to have news of you, but bad to hear that *What Is It the Mountains Say?* (A damn good title) has been returned by Knopf. I had the notion that Philosophical Library is a cooperative press. That's nothing against it if it is honest. As far as I'm acquainted with it Twayne isn't much of anything. I think your manuscript should be acceptable by a national publisher such a Knopf, but unfortunately Weinstock is right in saying they publish practically no verse now. Neither do any of the other big publishers. I can't imagine why Dutton keeps publishing me. As for that, I'd be glad to use whatever influence I might have with Dutton, if any, to get your manuscript read. I know for a certainty that their poetry schedule is filled until the end of 1957. They plan to publish my collected ballads then. Both I and Louise Nicholl, associate editor now, wanted the book scheduled earlier but the fall of 1957 was the best we could get. If as you say you want to get the poems published and on to something else you had best look elsewhere. Of course your poems are personal, I'm quoting back at you, but so is all the rest of poetry. It is true that your poems are naïve and child-like but in the best healthy sort of way. Whitman was as wide open as the plains of Texas but nobody denies now that he was a very great poet. You cannot be a great poet without first being a great person. Whitman,

Shakespeare, even Milton, though he was a crabbed old bastard. There is usually a flaw in the persons of great men but it is the greatness which counts … And all of this is platitude to you for you know it already. Anyway, if you decide to publish your poems yourself you might investigate Comet Press, Which does a good job of production. You can find the address in the *Saturday Review.* I've forgotten it. You might also investigate Alan Swallow, 2679 South York St. Denver 10. Alan publishes some books on a royalty basis under his own name as imprint and some on a coop or at the author's expense under the imprint of The Big Mountain Press. Alan's integrity is beyond question. He used to teach at the University of N.M. Also for a number of years at University of Denver. I've known him by correspondence ever since I was a striping, though there isn't much difference in our ages, as I recall. He had a Ph.D when he was just past twenty. I don't know what it might be, but if there is any service at all I can render toward getting your poems published let me know.

BYRON HERBERT REECE
ROUTE ONE
BLAIRSVILLE, GEORGIA

August 23, 1955

Dear Mildred:

Thanks for your letter. I won't be going to Emory in Sept. Probably not at all though I am committed for the winter Quarter. It appears I am less well than I was led to believe. I got up the other morning spitting blood to beat the devil, which is the first time I ever did that. So it appears "I done relapsed."

Well, to hell with it.

I thought the enclosed miniatures were rather attractively quaint. You can have 'em. You'll know whether they are "faithful Exposes" of habits and customs, etc et. I can't imagine why Stevens & Bro. ever had the interest to engrave them.

I enjoyed Hohn's visit. He sent me Caroline's memoir of Anderson. It might very possibly go with a magazine like *Georgia Review* if it were a little more severely edited and dates supplied.

I don't know when I'll see you over there. It taxes me now to walk across the living room. I said something to YHC about giving 'em my books and they seem interested, though they probably aren't. Anyway they won't want them before the library is ready for use again which will be somewhat later. How much God knows. I'll haul off and give them to Hall C. Lib if I get in the right mood. Union County ain't interested in anything but petty politics.

I read *Summing Up* a good many years ago. I like it for the same reasons you do plus the statement somewhere that the judge in Old Bailey should be required to keep a roll of toilet paper on his desk along with the flowerpot to remind himself that he is human like the men he judges.

Best to you all.

Byron

BLAIRSVILLE, GA.

September 17, 1955

Dear Elliott:

Thank you for all the reviews. Of all those you have sent I like Coleman Rosenberger's in the *NY Herald Tribune* best. (I am a little amused at the way the photo reproduces there, it makes me look like Fulton J. Sheen and I suppose both of us should cry: "The fiend forbid!") Ralph Morrissey devoted a good bit of his column "Under the Green Lamp" to me on September 4th. Ralph McGill sent me a tear sheet of that. You could have it, but I'm assuming the *Nashville Tennessean* sent copies to you.

I note what you say about the *Savannah Morning News* review. I've always liked Mrs. Hunter, whom I met briefly once, and do appreciate the space the *News* has always given me. I don't agree with her reading of *Hawk*, nor that the need for the book is past. People can be remarkably literal-minded. Nothing has changed in the situation that caused lynchings in the past, and until the situation has been changed there is always the danger of a flare of rage leading to such violation as I described. There is, however, nothing in the book to prevent a symbolic reading. The denial of human dignity to any group can maim, violate and emasculate. And I think there is a definite affinity between the emotionalism of sex, religion and physical violence. Well, anyway the book is out and will have to do its work as it was constructed.

No, you wouldn't know *The Southerner*. It is a monthly newspaper published by the Union Assembly of the Church of God. It is less than a year old, reaches a number of readers since it is the official organ of that religious group and is pro labor and so reaches a fairly large segment of labor, too. Don West, as you probably know, has been accused of being a Communist. I am not impressed. If I held him responsible for an early flirtation with the Communist Party I'd also have to hold most of the intellectuals responsible for the same thing. I have no sympathy for the Communists. I have no sympathy for the witch-hunters either.

Hope you succeed in blasting a review out of the *Times* or *Tribune.*

Thanks again, and I'll be looking for you in October.

Sincerely,

Byron Reece

BYRON HERBERT REECE
ROUTE ONE
BLAIRSVILLE, GEORGIA

Sept. 17, 1955

Dear Mildred:

Thanks ever so much for the paper. It arrived the day following my birthday so it counts as a birthday present. Did you know your ancient friend was 38?

I'm all balled up trying to keep up with things. I'm not making much headway and am inclined to throw in the sponge. (I know I shouldn't is—flirt this script on you, but my dad is sick and doesn't like to be disturbed at this hour of the night by the clatter of the typewriter.) I think everything converges on me at once, as far as correspondence goes. I've heard from everybody all at once, and, oddly enough, mostly not connected with the novel.

As for the novel, I think every newspaper in the country must have reviewed it last Sunday. My publishers have had a change of heart and are sending me the reviews as they come in. It truly is enlightening to see what you meant when writing a book by reading the reviews. Most of them are favorable, all I have seen as a matter of fact, though two or three Southern Reviews have been tongue-n-cheek. I got a big kick out of William Goyan's review in the *N. Y. Times.* He said the novel is "a cold and savage poem, a marked drunk show of human ignorance and violence." The *N.Y. Herald Tribune's* treatment was the best yet, though the *Boston Geabin* runs it a close second. I hope somebody will send me a copy of the *Gainesville Times* review. Otherwise I'm not likely to see it. In that regard, I'm sorry they didn't send the novel to you for review. And further, Dutton's publicity director says he sent out a biographical sheet with the novel wherein he "leaned so heavily on Mrs. Greear's *Gainesville Times* story" he felt like paying you royalty. I wrote him you'd probably have no objection to receiving royalty (that looks like crowned heads were coming visiting-I mean the 10% kind.)

Well, this fountain pen makes me feel awfully inarticulate. I should have known I wouldn't get a satisfactory letter written this way. But it does serve to send you my thanks.

Best Always,

Byron

******POSTCARD ATTACHED AT BOTTOM******

Dear M:

The Ms. has arrived and I'll read it carefully, as soon as possible. I'm presently occupied teaching Am. Lit. to high schoolers at YH. Summer ain't no time for learning, except how to play the role of coal, lying on the lap of earth almighty, drinking the sunshine in. I should be able to read with some awareness this weekend.

Best,

Byron

October 17, 1955

Dear Mildred:

Thanks a heap for the picture of the Hall County Library Exhibit from the *Times*. I know it was largely through your articles and Philip's photo that such interest on their part came about, and I do appreciate the good offices of you both.

I doubt that I could pick out a best year of my life. I could easily pick out a worst one, and that was 1954. That was a terror, believe me. This has not been a good one in particular … I've mostly wasted it completely. Do you know I have not written a word since November of last year, of poetry that is? I haven't written a word of prose since the last day of December last year when *Hawk* was completed. It doesn't worry me in particular. I've had dry periods before. The longest from the time *Bones* was accepted through 1947. I didn't write a thing that was worth a damn in that four-year period. Since that time I have written and published five books. I suppose if I regain enough energy and don't have too many interruptions I'll get back into kilter after a while. The Emory thing coming up in the winter is decidedly an Interruption. Nevertheless it may possibly be a good thing, aside from the fact that it will improve my financial status, for I can't seem to get on with anything now. I may revert to writing out of pure disgust when the course is over.

The reaction to *Hawk* has been generally favorable to judge by the reviews. I've seen some forty or more and all have been favorable with one or two exceptions. It was given the lead review in the *Los Angeles Times* on Oct. 9th. Paul Jordan-Smith who reviewed it there, he's lit. ed., voted for it in the *Saturday Review* Poll of Best Books for fall. Today I got a letter from Jerry Wald of Columbia Pictures asking if I had any ideas suitable for filming. Hawk would make a hell of a good picture, but I suppose it is too hot to handle. Besides, MGM has just filmed *Trial*, which deals with a race situation very similar, the suspect in that case being a Mexican boy. I doubt that I have any ideas that would interest Columbia but I'm going to outline one or two for Wald. I've got a marvelous idea for a sort of pantomime silent picture, but nobody but an experimental studio would have any interest in it. It is a pity most of my ideas are not adapted to commerce. I haven't the faintest notion how *Hawk* is selling, but I stick to the old saw, Blessed is he that expects nothing for he shall not be disappointed.

I know the children are enjoying the pony and sulky. When I was a kid I would have given my chance of heaven for a pony. The Fords of the construction gang, which built the Neel Gap road, had one when they lived where Vogel Park is now, and we rode it through the old fields where I was born, endlessly.

Best to you all.

Sincerely,

Byron

BLAIRSVILLE, GA.

November 18, 1955

Dear Elliott [Graham]:

Damn if I know what happens to my time here in this lazy world where nothing happens except lately frosts and freezes, but I see I'm late responding to your letters.

Thanks for the photos. I am glad to have the ones of you and Eva, with the figures of my dad and two of the dogs like small signatures hidden in the backgrounds. And even those of me. I hope I am properly indifferent to my own except in cases where the angle et cet make anatomical monstrosities beyond what nature did to me. Your lens reports me pretty straight, and so good for you. I don't know what possessed me not to get a close-up of you with your camera and your film. I'll do that the next time I see you. I'll be armed with my camera and we can try which is quicker on the draw.

I'm sinking deeper and deeper in the morass of the short story, learning all the things I didn't know about it, and was better off without. Maybe in the run of the next few months I will have taught myself how to write a short story. And by converse, how not to, and so come back to where I was. Anyway, the only thing I have in mind is called "*The Ailing and Passing of Brigid*" which bears no resemblance whatever to a short story. It will have to do with the ailing and … you guessed it, and the effect of her passing on the world which is represented by the diners and dancers gathered at the Blue Bar Grill. It will be a dilly and won't sell anywhere, and I don't know why I am taking up your time writing about it. I am afraid I'll have to get it out of my system, though, before going on to something else.

I sent Jerry Wald copies of the only two short stories I ever published and a copy of *Herbs* with some notes as to how I thought each might be adapted to the screen. Today I got a very nice letter acknowledging receipt of same together with a promise that as soon as he had read them carefully he would report his reaction. I tried to be intelligent about them. The only trouble is I don't really believe either of the three items is for the screen.

I am enclosing a copy of the review of *Hawk*, which appears in the Young Harris College paper. It is given more space than basketball, which is rather unusual. The editor of the paper is a perfectly beautiful boy about six feet two who approaches me with a reverence that is exasperatingly touching. I always have a desire to shock the young into a proper sense of reality. There are very few things in this life which one properly reveres, and a near-contemporary stringer-together of words is not one of them. I have, speaking of reviews, Gene Coughlin's from some Los Angeles paper, which you have probably seen. I take issue with his statement that *Hawk* is a pale copy of Faulkner, the old Marster. I have never been impelled to copy Faulkner. And as for that, in the matter of clarity with economy I can write rings around him.

The copies of *Hawk* will be most welcome when they arrive. As you will infer, they haven't. And Blood will wait: as a matter of fact it sometimes wears the disconcerting aspect of eternity. It will be good to see you in the shadow of it again (of Blood mt, Not it.) been awfully easy. Most college kids are so good, so eager, so susceptible, it's enough to break your heart.

I go back to work at Young Harris in June, if I survive till then. The goddamn dept of internal revenue robbed me while I was at Emory. I hope the bastards realize it was blood money they took from me; I spat on it. Seriously, I can't see taking over a fifth of one's salary simply because that person happens to be single. I wonder if the dept never heard of a case where a single person has as much responsibility as the bloke yoked with the unholy bonds of matrimony. I especially can't see taking money from citizens to spend on such tom foolery as the bomb tests now in progress. I don't give a damn, personally, if their bomb of "earthquake proportions" slits the old ball in two, but I don't want to help pay for it.

There's an old poem with the refrain:

Fara dara dino,

This is idle fino.

I guess that must be what most of this is.

Ever,

Byron

BLAIRSVILLE, GA.

April 4, 1956

Dear Pratt:

Thanks for all letters of yours, which I have not answered. I have often had it in mind to write to you, and I have thought of you often, but I am naturally lazy and I have been busy, and, as usual, short of energy. I concluded a quarter of teaching at Emory University on the 17th of March. It was a fairly interesting quarter of work, but hard, as usual. Teaching does take everything out of one, and I don't like teaching and I am not a good teacher, though better than some. Anyway, I usually am able to make contact with my students and they like me and I like them. I get the value of human contact from them, and get more deeply involved with some of them, but what they get from me God knows. I will teach again during the summer if nothing happens, at Young Harris College, a small college near home, and one I have probably mentioned to you before. I will work there at least through the summer session. I would like to come west, mostly to meet you and to see the country; the Georgia air seems to suit TB well enough. I'm in fair shape as regards that, only have to be careful, always have to be careful and worry about whether or not I'm being careful enough until I reach the point of to hell with it and break loose, but I don't want a teaching position with much responsibility. (Here where I'm known I can pick a light schedule, if there were such a thing in teaching. The trouble is I worked hours and hours on each day's assignment then met with students informally till all hours and then had a social obligation with a faculty member or some such almost every night, until I was worn to a husk. When I had a free weekend I grabbed a fifth of Calvert and fled home to the mountains.) But I don't suppose I'll ever be able to afford to travel out your way unless I do get a job of some kind in that country. Do you know of any openings where there is little physical exertion required and not much more intelligence? I'm getting awfully lazy intellectually, too. I sometimes wonder if I'll ever have the guts to write anything else of any consequence. Maybe, maybe not, I can't feel that it much matters. I don't much agree with you about learning how to live. Or to put properly, I think we have less and less to live for as we grow older and should by reason of experience know better how to live. At this point it doesn't matter a great deal to me whether I live or die, and the sad fact about it is that I don't feel at all sad about it, I am merely indifferent.

But as for writing, I'm enclosing some copies of some reviews of my latest book. It was published last September and received a great deal of notice in the press, mostly favorable, but hasn't been selling at all well. I suppose it is enough to scare readers away to learn that I'm a poet. If I may say so, *The Hawk and the Sun* is a damn good book, though not primarily a race study as most of the reviewers would have it. I liked Goyen's review best of all I saw. I have a contract for a new novel, with the deadline less than a year away, but I haven't written a word of it yet. I sometimes consider buying back my contract and calling the whole thing quits. As I said before I am lazy, and as you will infer, I am discouraged by the lack of a public large enough to mean anything financially. Once I could write and earn my living at something else but I don't have that kind of energy anymore. Nor the kind of care for writing that makes one do it in spite of hell and high water, to coin a phrase (to coin a phrase.) I always go off on this kind of tangent, sometimes for years, but so far I have always gotten around to writing something. Perhaps I will again. Dutton won't press me about the deadline. And when the book is published they won't advertise it either. But I don't suppose it would make much difference if they did. The publication of my Collected Ballads is set tentatively for 1957. I have the Ms. almost complete, though I will probably get a bug and go through it and make all sorts of revisions and have to do the whole thing over again. My *Season of Flesh* was listed by some reviewer as the best book of poetry of 1955 in the *Saturday Review's* poll, or so I hear. I have been absent from the *SR's* subscription list lately.

I am looking forward to the completion of your anthology. When it is ready please send me a copy and I'll send a check in return. I'll do what I can to see that it gets circulated, though of course that will be little, I'm afraid. At least I won't lend others my copy. I'm always enraged at people who write me and say "You'll be glad to know that I have loaned my copy of your latest book to umpteen different people." I'm never glad at all. (Except that those umpteen have read my book.)

It is spring here now with the service trees and the red buds in bloom. A little earlier the wild plums, with their bittersweet odor, and of course the peach and the pear. At this time of the year I always get nostalgic for eternity. Did I ever define nostalgia for you? It is the instantaneous recognition of our mortality. On another level, I am glad to be able to work in a garden this year (only remembering not to overdo it). I have a green thumb and my vegetables thrive, which fact cuts down on my grocery bill. For the past two seasons I've been denied the dirt delving. I like the feel of it.

Let me hear from you as often as convenient. I am always interested in what you are thinking and doing and writing and feeling.

Best wishes always,

Byron

BLAIRSVILLE, GA.

May 7, 1956

Dear Elliott:

The attached letter is self-explanatory. I would have sent it along earlier but I was waiting for the protected translation, which has not yet come through. I don't know what it says, but a friend of a friend of mine at Agnes Scott is making a translation. I suspect the article is pretty critical: I hear Europeans are that way. In America we like a thing or we don't, and we usually like what everybody else does. It gives one a charley horse gendering around to see what everybody else is liking. As Hank suggests there might be a possibility for promotion in the appearance of the article, but perhaps it may be too late now, and perhaps I should send it to a different department. If it's of any use, here it is, and you might return the letter if it is convenient.

Frankly, I am dubious of Dutton's interest in promoting marginal sellers. Perhaps from a business standpoint it is a necessary policy. I don't know. I do know that there was not a copy of any of my books in any bookstore in Atlanta with the exception of Rich's while I was at Emory. Through one thing and another I stimulated a good bit of interest in my books, but when Rich's sold out at the autographing, none were available to those who wanted copies. Perhaps it is the fault of the bookstores that copies are not kept in stock. But according to the good old American custom you have to sell to the retailers even those articles the customers want to buy. I guess it must be a matter of deep psychic import involved, like the oriental matter of "face." It's all beyond me. Anyway, I am disappointed in the sales of *Hawk*. I am disappointed that, so far as I know, there was never a single line of advertising of it. This, again, may be a justifiable business matter. If so I see no use of publishing anything but bestsellers. I see no use of writing anything but bestsellers. I guess in the coming age of automation there will be an IBM machine to turn out tomes bosoms, bedroom and bath, and we can all take a rest.

Today I got a dun from the bookkeeping department. "Since there is no royalty on hand," etc. I must have been owing the amount a long time. I've forgotten what it's for now. I'll settle up when I go to work again. I also intend to buy back my contract as soon as I can raise one hundred and fifty dollars, which I can possibly spare. I'm tired, I'm through, I quit. I'm aware that this fact is not going to break anybody's heart, thank goodness, not even mine. I'm truly beat and I just don't give a damn.

Emory was interesting and hard. I lost fourteen pounds and was spitting blood by the time the quarter was over. But I had a lot of fun. I'm the wrong kind of teacher for a course in writing. But I'm cheered by the thought that by the time the kids get out of college their intentions will probably get channeled away from writing anyway. I didn't get involved, though it would have been awfully easy. Most college kids are so good, so eager, so susceptible. It's enough to break your heart.

BLAIRSVILLE, GA.

May, June, that is, 17, 1956

Dear Elliott:

Thanks a lot for your letter and for the copy of Dave Steward's book. *Way of a Bucanneer* is a good swash-buckler, buckling and swashing in just the right places. As a literary effort it ain't worth a damn, as probably nobody knows better than Dave. But don't quote me. And I know that the bucanneers of a publisher's list have their places, too. They're just not my meat. (And incidentally I guess you had better give one of them n's the value of a c and shunt it around a little. I never could spell foreign words and I know darn few natives.)

There was a pretty good book by William Maxwell, I think, published several years ago. It was called *The Folded Leaf.* I never did discover why. Anyway, the boy who cut this throat discovered that each man has his limit. Beyond this wall I may not go, each man says to himself somewhere along the line. Well, I've just reached my wall. I've reached the absolute limit of my energy. I couldn't do more than I'm doing if my life depended on it. That's all there is to it. I think perhaps you might be right in thinking things would work out in time. But waiting it out is a luxury that I can't afford anymore. Success and I just missed connections somewhere along the line. Well, to hell with it. I've got to eat. I don't like to be hungry. So I'll meet my English classes as long as I can.

I started Summer school more than a week ago. I have a high school level course in Am. Lit. (Young Harris includes two years academy.) I have a small group of appealing little illiterates. But, God, no wonder we have a culture geared to twelve-year-old minds. The high schools these days teach nothing. But nothing. I hope John Dewey spends eternity in hell watching imps cut out paper dolls while Wm. Kirkpatrick plays ring around the rosey with assorted devils on a bed of live coals.

I'll be free for about six weeks after the 18th of August. I hope you can plan to come to Blairsville while I'm between terms. I already feel that I could spend some days just sitting without doing anything more energetic than reaching for a glass of cold Taylor now and then.

Let me hear from you.

Faithfully

BLAIRSVILLE, GA.

May 5, 1957

Dear Pratt:

Thank you for your letter of April 3. I had not seen the article from *Trace*. Thanks for sending it.

For the past year, almost, I have been teaching English, of one kind and another, at Young Harris College. I think perhaps I have mentioned the fact here at Blairsville. It is mostly a dead rind, but one must live. The quarter at Emory in 1956 was fairly interesting, but hard. I was not cut out for a teacher, though I'm a better one than a lot of them I've encountered, if for no other reason than the fact that my mind is not closed and I am not a social fossil. (By social, I mean in the sense of men's living together. I am not a "social" anything.)

The school year will be over on the last day of May. I look forward to that date with a great deal of anticipation. I have just been awarded a second Guggenheim Fellowship, and I want to get to work on a literary project now. I have written nothing since the last day of 1954, when I completed the manuscript of *The Hawk & The Sun*. I doubt if I ever write much more poetry. I don't feel it anymore. My new project will be a novel, called *The Ax and The Sword,* and will concern itself with the settlement and development of the Southeast, specifically my own mountain section of Georgia. The ax cleared the wilderness, the sword slew brothers in the civil war. I can't help getting symbolic when I think of a story. A story for its own sake is not worth telling.

It would be good to hear more from you. I always thought we might meet sometime, but now I don't know. I have lost contact with most of the people who meant anything to me in earlier years. I have now stopped getting involved with people. In the words of the prologue of *Hawk* etc. I am committed to the knowledge of the insuperable separateness of the individual. It was better, though, when an illusion spanned the distance between me and other individuals.

Perhaps someday I'll have enough time and energy to get a consistent letter together.

Best,

Byron

HUNTINGTON HARTFORD FOUNDATION
2000 RUSTIC CANYON ROAD
PACIFIC PALISADES, CALIFORNIA

June 24, 1957

Dear Pratt:

I am here at the Huntington Hartford Foundation for the summer, and perhaps for the fall and into the winter, too. I am working on a novel about the settlement of the north Georgia country, to be called *The Ax and the Sword.* At least that is the project I am here to work on. So far I have done no actual work on the novel. I have not been idle; I've worked on a few poems and have written some stuff based on the experience of coming out, etc. I arrived on the 19th and am not fully settled in yet. Perhaps I never will be. It remains to be seen.

But since I am this close it seems to me it would be a pity not to visit with you if there is the possibility of that. I could invite you here, but only for the day, and then we would have to go outside for meals. It's about twenty minutes from here to Westwood Village and there's no transportation out except occasional runs of the Foundation station wagon. Would it be possible for me to visit you in Berkeley on some weekend? How far is it from here to there, anyway? There is no map here and I have never been in Berkeley.

Let me know what you think, and let me hear from you anyway. I feel pretty isolated here. There are several other Fellows at the Foundation, musicians, artists and writers, but so far I have found no one suited to my temperament. I hope to get a good mass of work done while I'm here, but meanwhile I'd like to make contact with a fellow human being now and then. We have been able to communicate in the past.

Sincerely,

Byron Reece

HUNTINGTON HARTFORD FOUNDATION
2000 RUSTIC CANYON ROAD
PACIFIC PALISADES, CALIFORNIA

July 13, 1957

Dear Philip and Mildred:

I've been here nearly a month now, without any spectacular results. The flight out was fine. It was smooth all the way despite the fact that it is summer and the heat boils up off the countryside usually making for rough air. John and Ruth met me at the airport and the fact that I have known them a long time made me feel pretty much at home. Several Fellows have arrived since I did and I notice that though nothing is left undone for their convenience and comfort the reception is not particularly friendly. Not unfriendly but matter of course, which is not quite enough when one is getting into a new situation. The Foundation itself is in a wild canyon, in the middle of Los Angeles (which also includes a desert and two national forests). The deer come down to browse almost every day. I have photographed two from my studio, one not six feet from my bedroom window. The 'coons visit us nearly every night. The foxes bark from the walls of the canyon, and now and then a mountain lion lets loose a scream. It is hard to believe, but it's all true. Once one of the fellows saw an armadillo in the canyon. There are plenty of rattlesnakes, and the other day I was riding with an artist and we saw a snake in the road. He got out and caught it by the tail. It was a bull snake about six feet long. The human animals are all nice enough. Ernst Toch is here. He wrote the opera *The Princess and the Pea* among many other things. Also Eric Zeisl, a composer who does scores for the movies when he gets hard up. There are now four artists, six writers, and none of whom you have ever heard except possibly Theodore Pratt who has written twenty-six books including *Seminole* and *The Barefoot Mailman*. But we are all writing books, so perhaps you'll hear of us later. There are two sculptors. An English girl by way of Philadelphia who has an accent wondrous to behold, and a beautiful boy from Ohio who is a very nice guy all the same. I guess that is about all of us. Our cook and butler are Hungarians, He has a couple of Ph.D's and none of us dare offend him by being late to meals and that kind of thing. I have done a good deal of work, but practically none on the novel. This is not my climate, really, but I might as well soak up the atmosphere and charge it to experience and get what I can done. My time has been extended for three months, so I will not be home until just before Christmas. The director, John Vincent, has no more respect for his own rules than is to be expected. I have been to Hollywood to see *The Matchmaker* by Thornton Wilder, but otherwise I have stuck pretty close to the Foundation. Los Angeles is a true horror these days, very much worse than it was when I was here before. It is smogged in nearly every morning, and the traffic is practically bumper to bumper all day and every day, and I don't see how the inhabitatnts keep from going out of their minds. The city (generic) has reached its apotheosis; it is already insane.

Love,

Byron

July 14, 1957

Dear Pratt:

I've meant to write and perhaps even visit before this time, but there is so little of time for doing things, even when it seems to drag, that one is never up with work. I am at the moment engaged on something, a Christmas cantata with John Vincent who is the director of this place and Music Prof at UCLA, which should be completed in about two weeks. Then I want to come up for a couple of days at least. Maybe a week if I can spare the time and you can put up with me.

I have done nothing on my novel beyond a little character sketching since I've been here. This is not my climate really. I think I'll have to get back on the ground, North Georgia and vicinity, before I can do much with the novel. Meanwhile I'm doing some other things, a few poems, getting back into the habit of writing verse, which I have been out of for more than two years, almost three now. Also a thing on my flight out, which is of no particular importance, and a running record of my days here. I lost a lot of good experience, though it was deathly bad, when I was in the hospital by not writing it down.

At the moment I am feeling rather stifled with things here. I don't like the daily contact with the others, though they are all good people and I'm forced to see them only at meals. There are times when I hate solitude, but on the whole a good deal of solitude is necessary to me, I mean in blocks of days and days, if I am to get any real work done. I have a habit at home of getting in my car and driving aimlessly for hours, usually at a high speed, which may not be a sensible thing to do but I get a sense of release from it and it clears things for me. I also of late years have developed the habit of at times getting systematically and solitarily drunk. All this I could do at home without interference or comment from anyone. Besides of course I am a rural person. Small towns and middle-sized towns are all right, but cities are simply and indisputably insane. This is an isolated place, but to remain here is to be hog-tied. One has to go into town for anything except meals, and it is simply appalling how much time is wasted in getting into the mad hive and out again for so small an item as a bottle of bourbon or so necessary a service as a haircut.

I won't of course be here long enough to let things bother me much, till December 20 at the outside; I may capitulate before then, but I am an impatient person in a way though I also have the patience of Job when I'm forced to have.

All this is not very enlightening. But I somehow resent splitting my life into working time and living time, I'm only working here. Whatever I mean by living includes meaningful contacts, as meaningful as one can manage, with other human beings. And freedom to move around in. I miss my students; I have a knack for getting next to them, and I miss the open countryside of

Georgia. I can drive from home to Atlanta and back as quickly as I can go down town here and back, and its two hundred miles round trip to Atlanta. It's all fantastic.

But this is Sunday and Sunday is a particularly bad day for me. Let me hear from you, and I'll look forward to visiting with you as soon as I clear the cantata work.

Faithfully,

Byron

Glossary

Who's Who Among Recipients

George Broadrick
A student friend of Reece at Young Harris College. He and Reece were fellow members of "The Quill Club," a literary group at the college.

Pratt Dickson
A younger writer from South Carolina who had read some of Reece's poems and looked to Reece as a mentor. They never met in person.

James Gaskins
A fellow student friend of Reece at Young Harris College and a member of "The Quill Club." In later years Gaskins became Chairman of the English Department at the University of North Carolina.

Elliott Graham
Publicity Director for E.P. Dutton, Reese's Publisher. Graham greatly admired Reese's work and was a strong supporter of Reece and his goals. Graham came from New York especially to visit Reece at his home in Choestoe Valley in October 1955 to interview Reece for the purpose of better publicizing Reece's novel *The Hawk and the Sun*. Graham was later a strong though unsuccessful advocate to the editorial board of Dutton for the publication of Raymond A. Cook's biography of Reece.

Phillip and Mildred Greear
Phillip was a close student friend of Reece at Young Harris College. Mildred Greear later married Philip and also became a friend of Reece. The Greears and the Reece family have maintained a close relationship, and it is through Philip and Mildred that many facets of Reece, man and poet, have been made available.

E. V. Griffith
Though they never met in person, Griffith was a long-time correspondent from California who had initiated correspondence with Reece concerning their common interest in writing.

Leon Radway
Fellow student at Young Harris College. Reece's thirty-two poems in the anthology *The Lyric Poets* were dedicated to Radway.

CPSIA information can be obtained at www.ICGtesting.com
Printed in the USA
LVOW13s0150050514

384425LV00003B/5/P

9 780877 973744